Anonymous

The All-Round Route Guide

Second Edition

Anonymous

The All-Round Route Guide
Second Edition

ISBN/EAN: 9783337147679

Printed in Europe, USA, Canada, Australia, Japan

Cover: Foto ©Lupo / pixelio.de

More available books at **www.hansebooks.com**

THE
ALL-ROUND ROUTE
GUIDE.

THE HUDSON RIVER; TRENTON FALLS; NIAGARA; TORONTO; THE THOUSAND ISLANDS AND THE RIVER ST. LAWRENCE; OTTAWA; MONTREAL; QUEBEC; THE LOWER ST. LAWRENCE AND THE SAGUENAY RIVERS; THE WHITE MOUNTAINS; ORTLAND; BOSTON; NEW YORK.

SECOND EDITION.

MONTREAL:
PRINTED BY THE MONTREAL PRINTING AND PUBLISHING COMPANY.
1869.

PREFACE.

We are aware that the country through which we propose to accompany the intending tourist is no new field, and that there is more than one guide ready to start with him for a by-no-means extravagant remuneration. Our charges, it is now almost unnecessary to state, are likewise on a moderate scale; and we trust we shall not be found an unpleasant companion. Like the Verger, of historical fame, in Westminster Abbey, we shall point out all objects of interest; but, unlike him, we shall not hurry on at a breathless speed, —our pace will be as moderate as the rate of knots per hour performed either by rail or river steamer, will allow; and those who take us for a Cicerone will, we hope, enjoy the time and opportunity, as occasion offers, of thinking their own thoughts, and of giving way to any sudden outburst of feeling that either nature's grandest aspects, or the small asperities we shall occasionally bring our moral shins in contact with, will be calculated to call forth.

The unqualified success which has attended the publication of the *All-Round Route Guide*, and the many eulogiums it has drawn from an appreciative public, have prompted the Proprietors to make several important alterations in the work.

Suggestions have been received from friends, dating from different points along the route, and where throwing new information in the way of the traveller, they have been adopted,—thus forming valuable additions to the text. At the same time a series of photographic views from the admirable camera of Mr. Henderson, of Montreal, taken expressly for this work, will form an important and beautiful feature in the new edition. Six pages of the work will be found thus illustrated, comprising eleven different views of the most interesting and important points visited on the journey, so that when no longer in use as a guide,—the *All-Round Route* " vade mecum,"—will still possess a charm which will entitle it to a place where more ponderous guides have no room.

THE HUDSON RIVER.

THE scenery of the Hudson River has been so often written and talked about, that all who have never yet passed up its varied course will, we presume, on starting on a trip of pleasure, endeavor to make acquaintance with a district that is not only beautiful to the eye, but has been the scene of many of those bloody actions between the Americans, while yet struggling for their independence, and the troops of Great Britain, before the yoke of sovereignty had been fairly broken.

We imagine, therefore, that this trip will be taken by daylight, and we recommend to the notice of our readers the splendid steamers "C. Vibbard" and the "Daniel Drew," of the Day-line of Steamers. These are indeed floating palaces, for the speed and arrangements of the vessels, and the luxurious fittings of the saloons, are not surpassed by any other line of boats on the continent. The People's Line of Steamers —the "St. John" and "Drew,"—are equally fine boats ; but, as they make the trip by night, the scenery cannot be enjoyed, though the comforts and even luxuries they offer must be appreciated. The day steamers leave the wharf at Desbrosses Street every morning at 8.00, call at the foot of 34th Street a quarter of an hour later, and run up the 150 miles of the Hudson by 6 o'clock in the evening. A most comfortable meal can be obtained on board these boats; but as much beautiful scenery, to say nothing of the countless picturesque boats which add so much to its charm, would be missed during the consumption of this meal, we would recommend our readers to fortify themselves as to the inner man, before they come on board, and take up their position on the main-deck, under the grateful covering of the awning, and make good use of their eyes, while the varied scenery of the river passes in review or panoramic order before them.

For the first twelve miles of our upward journey, we skirt along the ISLAND OF MANHATTAN, upon which the City of New York is built. One of the first objects of interest we see on the right hand, is the handsome stone edifice of the New York Orphan Asylum, where nearly 200 children of both sexes are clothed, fed, and taught, and ultimately assisted to find respectable employment in the world. The happy and contented looks of these poor children are, perhaps, the most satisfactory proofs of the success of this inestimable institution, which, founded in 1806, by several benevolent ladies has, little by little, progressed, until we find it now occupying the stately and comfortable house whose gardens stretch down to the very edge of the water.

On the opposite side of the river, we pass by the yet picturesque villages of HOBOKEN and

WEEHAWKEN. We say yet picturesque, as their close proximity to that city of cities, which is daily travelling onwards, would make one imagine that the villas and street palaces of its merchants would spoil their rural beauty; but this is not so. How long this state of things may remain it is impossible to conjecture, as lager bier saloons, pleasure gardens, and restaurants are daily been raised here.

Crossing again to the other side of the river, we see a shabby looking village called MANHATTANVILLE, chiefly occupied by a class of people, who certainly have not got the knack of making places they inhabit, look either clean or comfortable; the close connexion which notoriously exists between the lower orders of the Irish and the denizens of their pig-sties may have something to do with this want of cleanliness.

Just above Manhattanville is Trinity Cemetery, where, among many others, lies Audubon, the celebrated naturalist, who has also given the name to a small village of about twenty or thirty acres where he used to live, but which, since his death, has been cut up into building lots, and still retains the aristocratic name of Audubon Park. Just beyond this Park a large building surmounted by a cupola, and having a tower at the south-west angle, may be descried among the trees. This is the New York Institution for the Deaf and Dumb, which, under the skilful management of Mr. Peek, is probably unequalled by any similar establishment in America. It stands in its own grounds of thirty-seven acres, and the terrace upon which the buildings (five in number, arranged in a quadrangle) are erected, is one hundred and thirty feet above the river. This Institution alone accommodates four hundred and fifty patients, and is only one more instance of the open-handed liberality and discriminating foresight of those in the State of New York, who do their best to alleviate distress in whatever form it may appear among their fellow creatures.

We here approach, on the same side, FORT WASHINGTON, or WASHINGTON HEIGHTS, as it is sometimes, and perhaps more appropriately, called. The ground is from five to six hundred feet above the river, and the view from this spot is exceedingly fine, the eye being able to trace the windings of the Hudson River northward for many miles, whilst southward the great city we have just left, with its suburbs of Brooklyn and Jersey City, can be plainly seen, though ten miles off.

We now leave the Island of Manhattan behind us, having by this time passed abreast of the SPUYTEN DUYVIL CREEK, which separates the Island from the rest of the State of New York. The Hudson River Railroad crosses the creek by a long bridge, laid upon piles, and a station, called after the name of the inlet, is immediately on the other side of the bridge. On the opposite shore of the river, that singularly beautiful formation of rock, called "THE PALISADES," commences about here. They extend for nearly thirty-six miles, and are considered by many as the most interesting feature in the scenery. Commencing at Hoboken, this threatening ridge can be discerned as far as the Hook, towering as it were over the river to a height varying from three to five hundred feet, and the apparent columnar structure, as seen at a distance, forcibly reminds one of the far-famed Fingal's Cave.

About two miles and a-half above Spuyten Duyvil, the tourist will perceive a handsome stone castellated building. This was erected by Mr. Edwin Forrest, the eminent tragedian, as a residence, and is called Fonthill. It has now changed hands, and is a portion of the building belonging to the Convent and Academy of Mount St. Vincent, as the surrounding neighbourhood is called, having a station on the Hudson River Railway. Two miles higher up, we come to the flourishing village of YONKERS, near to which the little Sawmill River runs into the Hudson. The whole valley through which the Sawmill River runs is highly beautiful, and the angler will find it well stocked with fish.

Four miles more steaming through a strikingly picturesque country brings us to HASTINGS and DOBB'S FERRY, at both of which places the Railroad, which runs along the river, has stations. The division between the States of New Jersey and New York strikes the river on the left bank, just opposite Dobb's Ferry, and henceforth our journey is continued entirely through the State of New York.

We now approach a part of the river full of interesting associations to both the American and British nations, for it was about TARRYTOWN and TAPPAN, on the opposite side of the river, during the rebellion of 1789, that Major André, of the British Army, was hanged as a spy, after having been made fully acquainted with plans by which West Point could be seized by the British troops, Arnold, of Washington's Army, having turned traitor to his cause. Major André, who to the last maintained a character for personal bravery, terminated his life as a spy, whilst Arnold, after doing his best to deliver his country into the hands of their enemies, escaped death by placing himself under the protection of the British flag. Major André's body, after lying interred near the scene of his sad fate for forty years, was at last given over to his countrymen, and now finds a resting place among the great and the good of Great Britain in Westminster Abbey.

The neighbouring district of TARRYTOWN and IRVINGTON is rich in associations of that greatest of American authors, Washington Irving. About half-a-mile above Irvington, on the right hand side of the river, may be seen, peeping through the bower of trees that nearly hide it from view, the charming stone cottage, called "Sunnyside," the home of Washington Irving, and the place where most of his novels were written. The cottage was from time to time increased and improved whenever Irving had the means to do it, and it has now become naturally one of the chief objects of interest in the neighbourhood. Many other beautiful estates are to be seen around, and if time is a matter of no moment, we can well advise the traveller to stop here and spend some hours.

Half-way between Irvington and Tarrytown, and quite close to the river, we pass by a conspicuous house of white marble, built by the late

Mr. Philip Paulding, from the designs of Mr. Davis, an architect of some merit. Another mile and a-half brings us to Tarrytown, seeming to invite the tourist, with its white villas snugly perched on the hill-side, to tarry for a moment in its walls. We leave to philologists to decide on the derivation of the name, which by some is referred to the Dutch, who once were in force here.

At SING-SING, the next Station on the line, the tourist may possibly exhibit less anxiety to tarry awhile, for, as is well known, it is the seat of the Mount Pleasant Prison, belonging to the State of New York. The village itself contains about five thousand inhabitants, and is nearly two hundred feet above the river. The prison is built nearer the river; that for males being on the lower stage, whilst the building for females is higher up the slope. It has been completed since 1830, and can accommodate over a thousand persons, the buildings having from time to time been increased, as more room was needed.

Immediately opposite Sing-Sing, the Rockland Lake Ice Company have their depôt, and employ a large number of men each winter to cut and store ice for the coming summer's consumption in New York. It is curious to note that whereas New York is almost entirely supplied with ice from this neighbourhood, it is also supplied with water from the CROTON LAKE, which is hard by. This Lake is estimated to contain over six hundred million gallons of water, and (daily) fifty to sixty million gallons are contributed by it to supply New York with this necessary of life. The water is conveyed from this Lake, which is chiefly formed by a long dam being built across it, through an aqueduct thirty-three miles long, right up to New York. The entire cost of this aqueduct was twelve million dollars, and it is built of stone, brick, and cement, arched above and below, seven feet eight inches wide at the top, and six feet three inches at the bottom, the side walls being eight feet five inches high. A few more miles travelling takes us past the small village of HAVERSTRAW, which gives its name to the lovely bay, and then past a limestone quarry, extending along the bank for more than half-a-mile, and two hundred feet in height, and which must prove, from the number of men we can see employed on it, a very profitable speculation. Two miles further on, on the western side of the river, is GRASSY POINT, a small village where bricks are made; and, again, one mile higher up, is STONY POINT, where there is a redoubt of considerable extent,—another one on the opposite side, at VERPLANK'S POINT, guarding the entrance to what is called the "Lower Highlands."

Three miles above Stony Point is GIBRALTAR, or CALDWELL'S LANDING. DUNDERBERG MOUNTAIN rises its towering head almost immediately in the rear of this spot. Directly opposite is PEEKSKILL, a thriving village of some five or six thousand inhabitants. The river here makes a sudden bend to the west. This is called the RACE, and the scenery from here for the next fifteen miles is unequalled in beauty. On the right we pass by a rocky promontory, called ANTHONY'S NOSE, whilst on the left, or western side, we have the

Dunderberg Mountain already alluded to. Anthony's Nose is thirteen hundred feet above the surface of the river. The Hudson River Railway have had to tunnel under the bottom of this mountain for a distance of two hundred feet. On the opposite side of the river, a large creek can be seen, where vessels of almost any size could anchor. The entrance to this creek is guarded on one side by FORT CLINTON, and on the other by FORT MONTGOMERY—the two so close to one another that rifle shots could be easily exchanged, Fort Montgomery being on the northern side and Fort Clinton on the lower. Almost immediately under the shadow, as it were, of the former fort, lies the picturesque little island of IONA, belonging to Dr. C. W. Grant, and covered in the summer time with vines and pear trees, in the successful culture of which the worthy Doctor is supposed to be unequalled.

A little way above Iona, and but half-a-mile below West Point, we come upon the BUTTERMILK FALLS, caused by the flowing down of a small stream into the river below, and falling over the hill-side a hundred feet in as many yards. This fall, when increased by any late rains or swollen by freshets, well deserves the homely name by which it is known, the snow-white foam truly giving it the appearance of buttermilk.

Half-a-mile further up brings us to " COZZEN'S HOTEL DOCK" at West Point. Here the vessel on which we are travelling stops for a while, to land passengers who are anxious to remain a day or so at Cozzen's comfortable hotel. This, during the summer season, is a very favorite resort, and much crowded; travellers would do well to make use of the telegraph a day before hand to bespeak accommodation, or they may find themselves disappointed on their arrival.

One mile more brings us to WEST POINT itself, the most lovely of all the lovely spots on the river. It is well known that the great Military Academy is situated here. Space will not enable us to enter very fully into a description of the course of instruction pursued here, suffice it to say that the fact of a young man having passed through the course, is a clear proof of his being an officer and a gentleman in its broadest sense. The traveller may well pass a few hours in this locality, and if he should happen to be acquainted with any of the professors or cadets in the Military College, he will be enabled to go over the buildings, different galleries, &c., and judge for himself as to whether the instruction and discipline kept up is not likely to produce some of the finest military men that any European nation might well be proud of. Reluctantly we must draw ourselves away from West Point, and allow our steamer to plough her way once more along the flowing current, and between the shady and overhanging cliffs which give so much character to the scene at this spot. A very few revolutions of the wheel will bring us between the BOTERBERG MOUNTAIN on the western side, and the rock called BREAKNECK on the eastern bank, forming an imposing entrance to NEWBURGH BAY, from which a series of mountains, hills, and cliffs rise in succession until they seem almost to shut out all remaining nature, and to give the idea that one is at the bottom of a large basin, out of which there is no possible exit. CROWNEST is the principal one of these mountains, rising almost directly from the river bank, to a height of nearly one thousand five hundred feet. As the side of this mountain is entirely covered with foliage, the view of it in the summer time is most beautiful, and only to be exceeded by the sight of it in the commencement of October, when the fall tints are in their richest and most luxuriant profusion. Soon after passing between the two rocks, we come to a small town called CORNWALL, on the western shore. This is a place of very general resort in summer, and is much noted for its many pleasant drives and walks. Its nearness to the river and to West Point makes it a very favorite place for travellers to spend some few days, whilst many stay here a very much longer time during the warm weather.

Between Cornwall and Newburgh lies the once prosperous, but now sadly decayed settlement of NEW WINDSOR. It is now almost entirely a collection of small houses in a great want of repair. On the shore, but higher above it on the plateau, one can discover several large farms with comfortable houses attached, giving the idea that if there is decay below there is no want of plenty above. Leaving this tumble-down village either to get repaired or to fall into still greater decay, we will approach the more flourishing town of NEWBURGH, where the steamer stops for a few minutes to discharge some of her passengers and to take up others, and we will employ these few minutes in gazing at the substantial streets and houses of the town, which, by the bye, we should have designated a city, seeing that it boasts of a mayor and corporation of its own. The first settlement at Newburgh was made as early as 1709 by some emigrants from the Palatinate; since then, English, Irish, Welsh, Scotch and Germans have followed their example, but of all these varied nationalities, the Scotch have perhaps done the most towards making the place what it is. The brewery of Mr. Beveridge is situated here, where ales are made which are known all over the country, and, on a hot day, are certainly a most acceptable "beverage." Among the other large stores is an extensive flannel factory, in which a very large number of hands are daily employed.

Exactly opposite Newburgh is the more modest looking village of FISHKILL LANDING, from which place any traveller anxious to ascend the South Beacon hill can do so with the assistance of any of the boy guides to be picked up in the streets of the village; and let us tell the traveller that he had better avail himself of our advice and take a guide, or before he reaches the top he may have repented of not having done so, as it is quite easy to lose oneself in the numerous gorges and ravines that are about the summit of the Beacon. As this is one of the highest mountains about here, the view from the top is most extensive and interesting. Far up to the north the Catskill mountains can be discerned, while to the east the Shawangunk hills are to be seen. Southwards again Boterberg and Breakneck, already seen, guard the pass through which the river running at our feet finds its way down to the sea. But it is time that we should descend from our lofty position and go on our way up the river.

A broad rocky platform, jutting out into the river, cannot fail to attract the traveller's attention. This is called the Devil's Danskammer, or Dancing Chamber, and, down to a comparatively late date, was used by the Indians as the scene of some of their religious ceremonies.

For about the next five miles we steam on through pretty country, though without finding anything striking enough to draw attention, until we pass the little village of NEW HAMBURG, lying at the mouth of Wappinger Creek, which is navigable for some distance up. The railroad crosses the Wappinger by a causeway and drawbridge, and then pierces a promontory jutting out into the river, by a tunnel about eight hundred feet long. New Hamburg is a pretty little village, but nothing more. About a mile higher up, and on the opposite side of the river, is another small village called HAMPTON, then comes MARLBOROUGH two miles higher up still, with BARNEGAT nearly opposite, on the right hand side, and again MILTON LANDING two miles more on the left hand side. As these villages lie mostly on the high banks of the river, there is not much to be seen of them from the boats, but they act as outlets or ports to the country district lying behind them, and, judging from the numerous comfortable-looking country-houses in their immediate neighbourhood, must be tolerably thriving.

As already stated, these villages are hardly

important enough to require mention, but we now approach a town of some twenty thousand inhabitants rejoicing in the peculiar name of POUGHKEEPSIE, and nearly half-way between New York and Albany, being seventy-five miles from the former, and about seventy from the Capital of the State through which we are passing. It was formerly settled by the Dutch, towards the close of the seventeenth century, and is situated, like most of their river cities, at the mouth of a tributary stream or creek. The village, as it was then, has much extended, and now occupies the large open plain about two hundred feet above the river. The streets are broad, handsome, and well planted with trees, affording in summer grateful shelter from the piercing rays of the sun. Poughkeepsie is best known for the very excellent schools it maintains, a large boarding-school for boys upon College Hill being particularly renowned for the very excellent tuition imparted to the scholars. This building stands at the back of the city, about seven hundred feet above the river, and is a conspicuous object as seen from the water.

Six miles above Poughkeepsie, after a sudden bend in the river, we come upon some rocky and precipitous banks. This used to be called by the original settlers "Krom Elleboge," but has since been Anglicised into "CRUM ELBOW." Quite close to this, only high up from the river, stands the Village of HYDE PARK, called after a former Governor of the State of New York, Sir Edward Hyde, who, we regret to say, did not leave a very satisfactory reputation behind him; his tyrannical and unprincipled conduct is well known to all who have studied the history of New York when under British rule.

RHINEBECK LANDING lies about two miles away from the village of the same name, which was first settled by one William Beekman, a German, who came from the neighbourhood of the Rhine, and called the place partly in honor of his birthplace and partly after himself. Immediately opposite Rhinebeck Landing, across the river, is KINGSTON'S LANDING, a quiet little village, pleasant enough, but without any great activity apparent, though Kingston cement, which comes from here, is in much request. Between this and Hudson, fifteen miles off, we come upon a number of large substantially built and handsome country houses with lawns of smooth turf stretching down towards the river, and an air of luxury and wealth pervading the whole estates.

Six miles above Rhinebeck is BARRYTOWN, and four miles above Barrytown is TIVOLI, each of them possessing a station on the railroad, though, like many of the other villages, we have had a glance at, small and unpretentious, having, however, possibly a vast idea of their own importance, as a great deal of the farm and garden produce of these villages is sent up to supply the wants of the Fifth Avenue, and other districts of the great city. Opposite Tivoli, on the western bank of the river, stands a flourishing little village called SAUGERTIES, at the mouth of the Esopus Creek. This little place boasts manufactories of iron, paper, and whitelead, and a fine flagstone quarry. Two miles from Saugerties we pass MALDEN, which lies backed by the Catskill Mountains, and about ten miles on we come to the large village of CATSKILL. Passengers from New York by railroad who wish to ascend the mountains, must alight at Catskill Station, and cross by ferry to the village, and we sincerely recommend our travellers to avail themselves of this trip. They will find plenty of omnibuses and stages to take them to the Mountain House and the Clove, about twelve miles off. We shall not attempt to describe the scenery, which, at this point, must alone be seen to be appreciated. The Mountain House is built on a large platform, three thousand eight hundred feet above the level of the river, and can easily accommodate from two to three hundred guests. The view from this spot is of a most extensive character, and embraces a region of about ten thousand square miles in extent, portions even of Vermont, Massachusetts, and Connecticut being, on a fine day, plainly visible, whilst at least sixty miles of the Hudson River can be seen shining like a broad silver belt at our feet. Besides the Mountain House, the Falls must be visited, and we cannot do better than quote, and, what is more, endorse a paragraph which we find in "Miller's Guide to the Hudson River," and to which book we are indebted for much valuable and interesting information with regard to this locality.

"The odious showman spirit, that spoils so "many attractive places the world over, has "entered here, and turns the Falls on or off "according to the amount of sixpences forth- "coming from lovers of what, considering the "smallness of the stream when at its best, may be called pitcher-esque. But the Clove, or Cleft, down which the stream runs to the Hudson, is really wild and savage, and romantic enough for the most ardent lover of such rough scenery. These Falls are the outlets of two ponds far up the mountain, united and leaping down a perpendicular rock in two falls, one of one hundred and eighty feet, and another of eighty feet in height, and emptying through the Clove, a deep chasm, into the plain below."

Five miles from Catskill Station, on the eastern side of the river, we come to the large and handsomely built city of HUDSON, the chief town in Columbia County, one hundred and fifteen miles from New York, and thirty from Albany. The city is built on an eminence above the river, like many of the other villages we have passed in our course. The streets are wide and well laid out, and altogether the place has an air of thrift and prosperity. The principal street is called the Promenade, and laid out with trees and shrubs with excellent taste. One side is built with handsome houses, and the other is open to the river, and runs along the bank for nearly a mile. Any one anxious to pay a visit to the Shaker Village at Mount Lebanon had better leave the boat here and take to the train which leaves for Chatham three times during the day, and there the traveller will connect with the Boston and Albany Railway, and, after an hour's journey of twenty-three miles, will be landed at the SHAKER VILLAGE itself. Space will not allow an extended notice of this remarkable village, suffice it to say that cleanliness, and all the other cardinal virtues, reign paramount. Order, temperance, frugality, worship, are the Shaker things that strike one's senses on first arriving. Everyone here is free. No soldiers, no police, no judges live here, and among members of a society in which every man stakes his all, appeal to the Courts of Law is a thing unknown. Among a sect where celibacy is the first and principal code, it would seem as if such a society would of itself die a natural death; but yearly many fresh converts to the sect are made, and not only among the old and those tired of this world's pomps and vanities, but from the young and healthy of both sexes. Happiness, peace and plenty are so evident in all the villages of this most peculiar of all religious societies, that it is not remarkable to hear that at the census of 1860 the Shakers were discovered to number from six to seven thousand, and at the present day they count considerably more. Mr. Hepworth Dixon has lately written so fully about them in his interesting work, entitled "New America," that we should recommend the curious, or those who have visited any of their villages, to obtain the book and "read them up."

We must go back to our steamer at Hudson, however, after this digression, and before leaving this interesting town will tell them that the village opposite, which has the high-sounding name of ATHENS given to it (though for what cause we are ignorant) can be reached by a small steam-ferry. There is nothing, however, to reward the task of crossing, except perhaps in order to obtain a good view of Hudson; but as this can be done quite as satisfactorily from the deck of our steamer, we will presume our readers will not attempt the passage, but continue with us for the next thirty miles of our trip to Albany.

The light-house seen on the western side of the river on Four Mile Point (that distance from Hudson) marks the head of navigation for ships. About a mile higher up, on the same side, is COXSACKIE VILLAGE, the older portion is called Coxsackie Street, and lies on a large plain about a mile back from the river. NEW BALTIMORE and COEYMAN'S are two smaller settlements to the north of Coxsackie, with SCHODACK LANDING immediately on the other side, whilst four miles higher up is CASTLETON. Here the well known sand-bar, called the Overslaugh, is situated, a spot that has proved fatal to more steamboats and other vessels than any known place on the continent. The country just around here is flat, though apparently well cultivated. Soon after leaving this village we evidently approach a place of some importance, as the river has a busier look, and the banks are more thickly dotted with houses, and, after a few minutes' delay, we see in the distance the thickly built city of ALBANY, the Capital of the State, whilst the newly constructed railroad bridge, which spans the river immediately opposite the city, seems to bar any further progress in our floating palace. We have now really reached the end of our water journey, unless we wish to proceed as far as Troy, when a little steam tender will come alongside of our stately craft, and if any passengers intend to go on, and so reach Montreal without passing to

Niagara or Toronto, they can get on board, after having informed the Purser, who will see that their baggage accompanies them, and a half-hour's steam will take them on to TROY, where they can connect with the train leaving New York at 3.45 p. m., and reaching Troy at 10.00 p. m., engage their berth in the sleeping-car (which is put on to the train here) and find themselves in MONTREAL at about nine the next morning, after having enjoyed a refreshing and appetizing breakfast at the comfortable and handsomely fitted-up Restaurant in the newly-built Depôt at ST. ALBANS.

As we wish to take our travellers to Montreal by the round-about, but more interesting route *via* Niagara, we will return to where we left them on the quay at Albany, after having landed them from the steamer which we have been reluctant to quit. If they wish to go on to Niagara the same night, they have not much time to waste, as the train leaves the depôt as soon as the passengers from the boats can be got there; and after a night's travel of about three hundred miles they will reach the Suspension Bridge Station at seven o'clock in the morning. Before leaving Albany, we ought, in justice to the city, have drawn attention to the State House and the Dudley Observatory, about the only two buildings of any character in the whole place, and these two are not very likely to strike an observer dumb with admiration or astonishment on seeing them for the first time.

The view from the Capitol is doubtless very fine, as the whole of the city, and a large tract of the surrounding country, can be seen from this eminence. Some of our travellers, who wish to take things easily, and rest a night or some few hours at Albany, will find themselves very comfortably put up at the "Delevan House," kept by Messrs. Charles G. Leland & Co. They can then take the train on the New York Central Railway for Utica, en route to

TRENTON FALLS.

As these Falls lie only about seventeen miles off the line of railway, with a branch railroad right up to them, they ought not to be passed without a visit. We will therefore take our seats in the cars at Albany, by the train leaving at 7 a.m., change at Utica, and either hire a conveyance there to take us on, or get into the cars which connect with this train, and bring us to the Trenton Falls Station, a little after noon. The river forming the Trenton Falls is called the Canada Creek West, but, as this name is not euphonious, and rather a mouthful, the Falls have been named after the town or parish in which they are situated. There is no one special cataract at Trenton which in itself is pre-eminently wonderful, grand or beautiful. It is more the position, form and rapidity of the river, which give the charm, and make it considered by many as one of the most picturesque and lovely spots on the continent. As the usual passage for tourists is along the bed of the river itself, it can be understood that to see these falls aright there must not be too much water. The end of July, or the commencement of August, is the time to see them in all their beauty. In order to justify their name, there are two actual waterfalls here, which, within a few hours' journey from Niagara, or seen after that mightiest of all cataracts, would be merely considered as "squirts," but, when taken on one's way to THE FALLS, and viewed in connection with the surrounding scenery, are well worthy of the visit we propose to make. The banks of the river are thickly wooded on each side, with broken clefts here and there, through which the colors of the foliage show themselves, and straggling boughs and rough roots break through the high rocks, and add to the wildness and charm of the scene.

A comfortable hotel is situated in the village, where travellers can get all their wants supplied, and then take the cars at 3.45 p.m. back to Utica, where they can again join the New York Central line, and proceed *viâ* ROME, SYRACUSE, ROCHESTER and LOCKPORT on their way to Niagara. As we presume that this journey will be made without any further stoppages, we shall skip all these places, and merely say that they are the ordinary specimens of American towns, having broad streets, avenues of trees, large stores, and excellent houses, with an air of prosperity about the whole of them.

NIAGARA.

Having landed our travellers safely at the Suspension Bridge Station of the New York Central Railway, the choice of an hotel is the

1. *Suspension Bridge over Niagara River.*
2. *General View, Niagara Falls.*

matter of first and paramount importance. General opinion is much divided on this subject, many travellers asserting that the American side is the only one to stop on, and see the Falls, as the Rapids, the Terrapin Tower and Goat Island, are all to be reached from that side, and from that alone; whilst others take the broader view of the question that these comparatively gingerbread sights ought to give place to the Falls, and therefore the only place to obtain an uninterrupted view of the two mighty cataracts is from the Canadian side. We are inclined to endorse this opinion, and therefore, if our travellers will be guided by us, we advise orders being given to the driver of the carriage, that can be engaged at the Station, to proceed to the "Clifton House" on the Canadian bank, kept by Messrs. Bromley & Shears. We can justly speak most favourably of the creature comforts offered at this establishment, and when once ensconced in one of the cosy rooms overlooking the Falls, are sure that even the attractions of the "Cataract" and "International" hotels opposite would not induce the traveller to vacate it. The drive from the station to the "Clifton House" will necessitate the passage of the Suspension Bridge, and therefore, *en passant*, we will endeavor to give a short description of this wonderful triumph of engineering skill. The bridge is constructed for the joint purposes of road and pedestrian traffic, and for the Great Western Railway of Canada—the lower tier or floor being for foot and carriage passengers, whilst the upper portion is used entirely by the trains. There is a small toll levied on all passengers, and a custom-house officer will make a cursory and rapid search for any articles that, being liable for duty, are being carried across from the United States into the Dominion of Canada, or *vice versa*. Mr. Roebling, of Trenton, New Jersey, was the engineer of this Bridge, which, as the name implies, is constructed on the suspension system. The two towers supporting the entire structure, which is in one span (800 ft.), are about 80 feet high, and built on and into the solid rock; the aggregate length of wire employed is more than 4,000 miles, whilst the entire weight of the Bridge is 12,400 tons. From the centre of the tube or tunnel, the first view of the entire Falls can be seen, yet a mile and a-half distant : the never changing mist and spray dimly obscuring the view of the Horse-shoe or Canadian Fall. The drive is continued along the high bank overlooking the foaming, seething waters of the river which have so lately made their giant leap. Almost immediately under the Bridge can be seen, at a distance down of about 250 feet, the wharf from which the small steamer "Maid of the Mist," used to embark her passengers, before taking them up under the spray of the Falls. The successful escape of this little picture of a boat from the hands of the Sheriff, by taking the rapids and skimming through the whirlpool below, is now so much a matter of history that we will not weary our readers by detailing it again. There are several interesting legends and narratives connected with Niagara, but as our pages will not permit us to enter into all, or in fact any, of these stories, we would advise the purchase of some local Guide which can easily be obtained on the spot, and then the traveller can feel quite *au fait* to all connected with this interesting place. Our task is simply in as few words as possible to direct the tourist as to what to see, and how to see it. We will therefore imagine him to be standing in the balcony of the hotel overlooking the Falls, and explain to him that the right hand and larger cataract is the CANADIAN or HORSE-SHOE FALL, whilst the one nearer to him, on the left hand side, is the AMERICAN. The dimensions of the two Falls must necessarily be a matter of computation, and they are estimated as follows :

The American Fall, 900 feet across, with a drop of 160 feet.

The Canadian Fall, 1,900 feet across, with a drop of 156 feet.

GOAT ISLAND is the name of the tract of ground which separates the two Falls, supposed to have been so called from the fact of its having been a pasture land for goats very many years ago. The island is in the possession of a family of the name of Porter, who have allowed a small wooden bridge to be thrown across the RAPIDS from the main land. Access to the TERRAPIN TOWER, which stands out boldly almost on the very brink of the Horse-shoe Fall, can be gained only by passing across this Island, which is about sixty acres in extent, and nearly one mile in circumference. Visitors should not neglect to pay a visit to the Terrapin Tower. A view can there be obtained down into the very gulf of the Falls, and, with the sun shining on the water, the effect of the Iris or Rainbow is at times most striking. During the visitor's stay at the "Clifton House," or at any other hotel at Niagara, which we presume will, or ought to extend, over several days, excursions should be taken to the following places:—To Goat Island and the Terrapin, to the Three Sisters, and to the Rapids above the Falls. This can all be done in one day, and may be accomplished by descending the winding or zig-zag path which leads down to the river from the immediate front of the "Clifton House," thence by ferry across to the opposite shore, almost at the very foot of the American Falls, where a flight of 290 stairs leads to the summit; for those who dislike the ascent of so many steps, a car drawn up by a pulley, worked by water power, will raise the tourist up an inclined plane. A second day's excursion can be made to the WHIRLPOOL, three miles off the Falls, then to the "DEVIL'S HOLE," into which a stream, called "the Bloody Run," falls, (with a legend of course attached), and on to QUEENSTON HEIGHTS, the scene of an engagement between the Americans and the British troops in 1812, and where General Isaac Brock, and his aide-de-camp, Lt.-Col. McDonald, were both killed. A very handsome memorial pillar has been erected over the remains of these heroes, by the Provincial Government of Canada, surmounted by a massive statue of General Brock himself. This monument was partially destroyed by some miscreant of the name of Lett, but has since been repaired and much improved, at the public expense, as a fitting memorial of, and resting place for, the remains of these brave and devoted men. As this excursion must necessarily be made by carriage, we would urge our tourists not to neglect to make arrangements, on this and all other occasions, with the driver as to cost, before starting, or he may have cause to regret the omission. It is sad, we think, that even a spot like Niagara, the grandest of all Nature's efforts, should not be free from the spirit of grasping cupidity that is so noticeable at most other show places. To our mind, the tourist should be left alone, at such a spot, to enjoy nature in his own way, and not be pestered with touts who are anxiously endeavouring to screw a dollar out of the unfortunate sight-seer, either by getting him to have his photograph taken with the Falls as a background, or to purchase some stuffed bird or animal, or to obtain (on payment) an extended view of the Falls from the top of some Tower, or to take a drive to some out of the way place, or by any of the other thousand-and-one devices they have for "bleeding" the visitor.

A third day, or we shall say the last day, at the Falls may well be spent in seeing what there is to be seen of them entirely from the Canadian side. A visit must be made to TABLE ROCK, which is getting small by degrees and beautifully less, until shortly we fear there will be nothing left of it, for masses are constantly falling without any apparent cause, and larger portions that appear to be dangerous are as frequently being blasted by gunpowder, for fear of their falling unawares; after a view of the water from Table Rock, the visitor should go to the MUSEUM directly opposite, obtain a water-proof dress and a guide, and then descend by a circular staircase to a narrow ledge of rock which extends for some sixty feet under the mass of falling waters of the Horse-shoe Cataract. This is called the CAVE OF THE WINDS, and should be seen by any one with a strong nerve and a sure step, as there is some amount of risk attending the exploit. This is perhaps the last sight to be seen in direct connection with the Falls; we shall therefore return once more to our hotel, passing on our way the large and substantial stone house that belonged to the late Mr. Zimmerman, which stands adjoining the hotel, in its own park of about 20 acres. Mr. Zimmerman, the former purchaser, unfortunately lost his life in a railroad accident. It was at this house that the Prince of Wales stayed when he paid his visit to Niagara in 1860.

Before leaving this place, however, we wish to conduct our readers to one spot where, perhaps, of all others, the finest view of the waterfalls can be seen, and that is along the railway tract that lies at the back of Mr. Zimmerman's house, until an open spot is reached near a small reservoir, immediately above the Falls, and as we feel that our language is too poor to give any adequate idea of the grandeur of the sight before us, we will take the liberty of reprinting the actual words in which that greatest of living writers, Mr. Charles Dickens, has clothed his thoughts and feelings on his first visit to Niagara, twenty-eight years since, and which even now, with eight and twenty years' additional experience, he could not improve upon, either in force or poetic sentiment :—

"When we were seated in the little ferry-boat,

" and were crossing the swollen river immediately
" before both cataracts, I began to feel what it
" was : but I was in a manner stunned, and
" unable to comprehend the vastness of the scene.
" It was not until I came on Table Rock and
" looked—Great Heaven—on what a fall of bright
" green water !—that it came upon me in its full
" might and majesty.

" Then, when I felt how near to my Creator I
" was standing, the first effect, and the enduring
" one—instant and lasting—of the tremendous
" spectacle was Peace. Peace of Mind—Tran-
" quillity—calm recollections of the Dead : Great
" thoughts of Eternal Rest and Happiness—
" nothing of Gloom or Terror. Niagara was at
" once stamped upon my heart, an Image of Beauty
" to remain there changeless and indelible until
" its pulses cease to beat forever.

" I never stirred in all that time from the
" Canadian side, whither I had gone at first. I
" never crossed the river again ; for I knew there
" were people on the other shore, and in such a
" place it is natural to shun strange company.
" To wander to and fro all day, and see the
" cataracts from all points of view, to stand upon
" the edge of the great Horse-shoe Fall, marking
" the hurried water gathering strength as it
" approached the verge, yet seeming, too, to pause
" before it shot into the gulf below ; to gaze from
" the river's level up to the torrent as it came
" streaming down ; to climb the neighbouring
" heights and watch it through the trees, and see
" the wreathing water in the Rapids hurrying on
" to take its fearful plunge ; to linger in the

" shadow of the solemn rocks three miles below ;
" watching the river as, stirred by no visible
" cause, it heaved and eddied and awoke the
" echoes, being troubled yet, far down beneath
" the surface, by its giant leap ; to have Niagara
" before me, lighted by the sun and by the moon,
" red in the day's decline and gray as evening
" slowly fell upon it, to look upon it every day,
" and wake up in the night, and hear its ceaseless
" voice—this was enough.

" I think in every quiet season now, still do
" those waters roll and leap, and roar and tumble
" all day long ; still are the rainbows spanning
" them a hundred feet below. Still, when the
" sun is on them do they shine and glow like
" molten gold. Still, when the day is gloomy do
" they fall like snow, or seem to crumble away
" like the front of a great chalk cliff, or roll down
" the rock like dense white smoke. But always
" does the mighty stream appear to die as it
" comes down, and always from the unfathomable
" grave arises that tremendous ghost of spray and
" mist which is never laid, which has haunted
" this place with the same dread solemnity since
" darkness brooded on the deep, and that first
" flood before the deluge—Light—came rushing
" on creation at the Word of God." (*See Appendix*.)

TORONTO.

Our stay at Niagara having now drawn to a close, we must decide upon the route we shall take for TORONTO. There are two means of getting there, one by water and the other by land. On a sunny calm day nothing can be more pleasant than the water excursion, by the fine steamer "City of Toronto," which daily makes two trips each way across the Lake Ontario, between Toronto and Lewiston. If this route is decided on, the tourist will have to make for the SUSPENSION BRIDGE STATION, where, at 10.10 a.m., he will find the cars ready to take him on to LEWISTON, a small town on the American shore, almost immediately opposite to Queenston, on the British side, and to which place we have already bent our steps. From Suspension Bridge to Lewiston, the railway follows the course of the river, running along the high ridge overlooking the rapid stream, until we arrive at Lewiston Station. Omnibuses and cabs will be found in attendance to take passengers down to the steamer, which lies about half a mile off. Once embarked, we pass along Niagara River for about ten miles, the current still running very rapidly, until it finds its way into Lake Ontario. The first and only stoppage made between Lewiston and Toronto is at the Village of NIAGARA, 16 miles off the Falls. Passengers from the Clifton House can be brought by the cars down to this village without crossing to the opposite shore, and embark on board the "City of Toronto" here. Almost immediately after leaving Niagara Village, we pass between the Two FORTS, Niagara and Massasauga, the former garrisoned by American troops, and the latter by the soldiers of Her Majesty Queen Victoria. These two forts are so close together, that it is said, on a calm still night, the watchwords as given by the troops on changing guard, can be heard distinctly from one side to the other, across the water. From this point we strike out into the lake, and in the centre almost lose sight of the land behind us before we discern the city of TORONTO immediately in front of us. The view of Toronto from the water is very fine indeed, and, judging from the public buildings and wharves, shows it to be a city of some importance and prosperity. Before we commence describing it, however, we must return to Niagara to conduct our tourists who prefer the over-land route by the Great Western Railway. They also must make their way to the Suspension Bridge Station, and be there at 7.00 a.m., at 9.00 they will reach the prettily situated and thriving town of HAMILTON, built upon the banks of Lake Ontario, and the head quarters of the Great Western Railway of Canada, where the general offices, engine sheds and work shops are located. Forty miles more journeying brings the traveller to Toronto at 1.15 p.m., in time to catch the Royal Mail Steamer for Montreal, which leaves daily at 2.00 p.m. As we intend to recommend our tourists not to join the steamer until it gets to Kingston, we will give them the opportunity of paying Toronto a visit under our auspices, and acting on our general system, will at once direct them to an hotel where they can be comfortable. The "Queen's Hotel," belonging to Capt. Dick, and the "Rossin House," kept by Mr. Shears, divide between them the share of the visitors' patronage. With either, or both, the tourist will be perfectly satisfied, and though the "Rossin House," which was burnt down a few years back, has been again built and furnished in a sumptuous manner, the "Queen's" has also been lately redecorated and refitted. We shall, therefore, leave our travellers to choose for themselves, with confidence, as at either house they will be well cared for.

TORONTO is the chief city of Ontario, or Upper Canada, as the Province used to be called. A large sand bar, of about seven miles in length, terminating at what is called Gibraltar Point, forms, as it were, a well-sheltered and accessible harbor. The former name of this city was Little York, until 1834, when it was changed to Toronto. The streets are well built and broad, and some of the public buildings are remarkably handsome and merit a visit. The University is the chief attraction, and well supports its claim. The style is intended to be pure Norman, though in some of its minor details, modern requirements have made it necessary to depart from it. It stands in a large well-kept park, with avenues of stately trees leading into two of the principal thoroughfares of the city. The massive tower in the centre of the South façade is 120 feet in height. The Normal School and Trinity College on Queen Street West are both handsome edifices, which will well repay a visit. All these buildings, being devoted to educational purposes, prove Toronto to be second to no other city in the Dominion for the culture of the young. Osgoode Hall, where all the Courts of Law are congregated, is a handsome building enough outside, and inside the arrangements of the different courts, with spacious passages and galleries, are so perfect, that very many cities of more pretensions than Toronto can boast, would do well to copy. The Provincial Lunatic Asylum, the Elgin Association for improving the moral and religious condition of the colored population, and the Merchants' Exchange, should all be seen by the visitor. The English Cathedral, dedicated to St. James, and the Roman Catholic Cathedral of St. Michael, deserve notice. There are one or two pretty drives to be made out of the city, though the country around has not much beauty to boast of. The most attractive one, perhaps, is the drive along the road skirting the lake, which, on a fine day, is covered with boats of all shapes and sizes, from the Royal Mail steamers to the miniature skiff with its snow-white sails. As we have said, the Mail Line of boats leave the wharf daily for Montreal. Travellers can go on board, obtain their state-rooms, and make the passage of the Lake, if they prefer it ; but, as "variety is charming," and a change of conveyance is pleasant and even beneficial, besides which, of course, there is very little to see on the Lake, we think our tourists will be wise if they go as far as Kingston by the Grand Trunk Railway, and there take the steamer. They will not lose any of the scenery, as there is little or nothing to see along the banks of the Lake, and they will join the boat where the Thousand Islands begin, and can either go on direct to Montreal, or take the detour which we shall recommend to Ottawa, the Capital of the Dominion, and then proceed by the Ottawa River to Montreal. Let us presume then that this advice is taken, and our tourists seated in the handsome cars of the Grand Trunk Railway, steaming out of the Station at 6.30 a.m. or 6 p.m., as the case may be, trains starting at those hours daily. For a short distance, we run along the banks of the Lake, and then we lose sight of it altogether. There are only about three places of any importance between Toronto and Kingston, viz:—Port Hope, Cobourg and Belleville, and these can be described in very few words. PORT HOPE is a very pretty town, situated in a valley which the lake has here formed, the hills gradually rising one above another on the western side of the town. There are about 2,500 inhabitants. COBOURG is rather a larger place, seven miles off, and contains nearly 5,000 people. Here the train stops about a quarter of an hour, to give travellers the opportunity of demolishing the very acceptable meal that is ready for them in the Refreshment Room of the Station. A branch line runs up into the backwoods to Peterboro, and connects with the Grand Trunk here. The Wesleyans have erected a very handsome building, called Victoria College, and capable of accommodating about 150 students. Cobourg has also a fine town-hall and gaol, two very useful and necessary buildings in their respective ways. BELLEVILLE, the only other place we shall describe until we arrive at the end of our railway journey, is one hundred and twelve miles off Toronto, and forty-eight from Kingston; it is situated at the head of Moira River. The view from the surrounding country of the Lake is very fine, and the town itself from a distance looks remarkably well, as it covers the rising ground, while the steeple of St. Michael's Church, in the centre, gives an appropriate finish to the whole. About half-past two, either in the morning or afternoon, according to the time chosen for leaving Toronto, we reach KINGSTON, which was called by the Indians "CATARAQUI," and, as early as 1672, was a settlement of the French; 90 years later it fell into the hands of the English, in whose possession it has ever since remained. It is now a place of considerable commercial importance, being situated at the junction of the Bay of Quinté and Cataraqui Creek, whilst the Rideau Canal, which comes direct from Ottawa, falls into Lake Ontario at this point. The population is above 15,000 people. A large quantity of ships and boats are built at Kingston, and the town is rapidly advancing and improving. The Provincial Penitentiary is situated here, about a mile to the west of the city, and is a fine massive stone building; a high wall, with towers at each corner running round the place. The Market House, with the Town Hall above, surmounted with a cupola, is a conspicuous object from a distance.

THE THOUSAND ISLANDS.

The Royal Mail Steamer, which leaves Toronto on the previous afternoon at 2 o'clock, is due at Kingston between 3 and 4 the following morning. If we go on straight from the train to the steamer, we have a short drive to take from the Railway Station to the wharf, where we shall most probably

1. Thousand Islands, St. Lawrence River
2. Victoria Bridge, Montreal.

The Thousand Islands.

find the boat ready waiting; and, shortly after leaving Kingston, we shall be amongst THE THOUSAND ISLANDS, which stretch themselves along the centre of the St. Lawrence for a distance of forty miles. The entrance to these Islands is the termination of Lake Ontario, and the commencement of the River St. Lawrence. The stream here is about twelve miles wide, but so closely studded with islands of all shapes and sizes, varying from an acre to ten miles in length, that it is more like passing through a vast archipelago than following the course of a river. These Islands are believed to number between 1700 and 1800, and when once seen can never be forgotten. The water of the St. Lawrence is here of a bright green tinge, and beautifully clear. The Islands are nearly all rocky, and thickly wooded, and the water in places so deep that the steamer could easily run within a few feet of some of the cliffs. The fishing and duck-shooting among the Islands is extremely good, affording excellent sport both for the rod and the gun—indeed some of the largest Maskinongé ever seen out of the water have been caught here; and, as this may serve to whet the ardour or ambition of the angler, we can assure him, in the words of the old adage, "that there are as many good fish in the water as ever came out of it." These attractions, added to the charm of the exquisite scenery, should be sufficient to induce all of our tourists, if they will not even stay a few days among the Islands, at all events not to neglect to go down through them in one of the steamers of the Canadian Navigation

Company., BROCKVILLE is a prettily situated town, immediately at the foot of the Islands on the Canadian shore. To those who wish to stay here a few days for fishing or shooting, they will find themselves very comfortable at "Campbell's Hotel." The town was called after the General Brock whose grave and memorial we have already visited at Queenston Heights; it is well built on a series of ridges overlooking the river, with a population of about 5,500. PRESCOTT is the next place of any importance that we approach, and here we wish our tourists to land, in order to pay a visit to OTTAWA. This city, the Capital of the Dominion, is only a little more than fifty miles distant from Prescott, and the journey to it can easily be performed by railway in about three hours. We can confidently recommend this detour, not only on account of the claims of Ottawa itself, of which more anon, but because of the beauty of the Ottawa River, down which we propose to steam on our way to Montreal. Let our tourists therefore put themselves in our hands and they will be well repaid for the little extra time the trip may necessitate.

Having disembarked from our boat, we cross the wharf to the St. Lawrence and Ottawa Railway Company's Station, where we find cars waiting to take us on to the Capital of the Dominion. As we shall most probably have a few hours to spend here, we can supply them either by taking a walk round the town, which is situated in a very picturesque manner; or by crossing the river in the steam ferry "St. Lawrence" to the American shore at OGDENSBURGH. A railway runs from here to Rouse's Point, and is the most direct route between Boston, New York and Ottawa. Ogdensburg is apparently a very flourishing town, and shows in a marked manner the go-ahead enterprise of the American citizen in contradistinction to the more steady business spirit of the Canadian merchant, as evidenced by the town standing on the opposite shore of the St. Lawrence. Our spare time being now nearly exhausted, we will again cross the river, and take our seats in the cars for OTTAWA.

OTTAWA.

After a journey of about two hours and a-half over the 54 miles of the St. Lawrence and Ottawa Railway (which has lately changed its name from the Ottawa and Prescott) we shall be landed at the very unpretentious station of the Capital, at about five o'clock, p. m. Our steps will naturally be directed towards the "Russell House," under the management of Mr. J. A. Gouin. Here accommodation is provided for over 250 guests, and every comfort afforded at a reasonable charge, the whole arrangements being carried on under the personal supervision of Mr. Gouin, who will see that his visitors, during their stay under his roof, want for nothing. Ottawa (or Bytown as it used to be called) has been selected by Her Majesty as the new Capital of the Dominion, the chief seat of Government having for many previous years been settled at the cities of Montreal, Quebec and Toronto, in turns, for a certain number of years at each. This system was found to work very badly, and numerous quarrels arose between all of these cities, and the jealousy stirred up against the one that happened at the time to be favoured, made it necessary to choose some fourth place, and Ottawa was selected as being the most central and desirable that could be found. The Government buildings have consequently been erected here, and very much credit is due not only to the Architect who has designed these most beautiful buildings, but to the public spirit of the Legislature who have found the means for bringing the work to a successful termination. The Parliament Buildings with the Departmental offices, and the Queen's Printing House, occupy three sides of a square, on a bluff of ground overlooking the river, called Barrack Hill. They contain two Legislative Halls, one for the Senate, the other for the House of Commons, both being the same size as those provided in the English Houses of Parliament for the Lords and Commons, and, like their originals, very handsomely decorated and conveniently furnished. A large Library is also provided, capable of accommodating half a million volumes. The buildings are designed in the Italian-Gothic style, and constructed of stone found in the neighbourhood. When it is stated that the cost was $2,500,000, and the position almost unique, the tourist ought not to lose the opportunity of going there, as they alone are quite worth the few days' delay which must necessarily be devoted to the sight. The rest of the city, which is of course much increasing, and the whole of it nearly new, is very handsomely and substantially built. Sparkes Street, the scene of the assassination of the late Hon. T. D'Arcy McGee, is close to the Parliamentary Buildings and the Russell House. Like Quebec, Ottawa is divided into an Upper and a Lower town, the link between the two being the substantially built bridge spanning the Rideau Canal, which here falls into the Ottawa after passing through eight stone locks. This canal connects the Ottawa River with Kingston and Lake Ontario, through a series of lakes and streams, running in its entire length about 135 miles. The other chief attractions in the neighbourhood of Ottawa are the CHAUDIERE FALLS, considered by very many to rank next in importance, beauty and grandeur to Niagara. They stand, or rather fall, immediately above the city, at its western extremity, the width of the greater fall being two hundred feet, while its depth is forty—the boiling, seething, foaming character of the water giving name to the place. On the northern side is the smaller, or LITTLE CHAUDIERE, and here the waters, after their leap, seem to go into some subterranean passage, by which they are carried off until they appear again at a place called "THE KETTLES," half-a-mile lower down. Of course, the existence of such passages is a mere matter of conjecture, which we will leave to the study of Geologists, and others interested, to determine. Before leaving Ottawa, we ought to pay a visit to one of the Timber Slides, which are tolerably frequent in the upper river. One is erected on the northern bank, and we will here tarry for a moment whilst we watch the fate of one of those huge rafts of hewn wood down its headlong rush. These water-shoots are erected for the purpose of getting the fallen trees from the higher level down to the river, at the smallest possible cost, and wherever water can be obtained in sufficient quantity this has been done. Where the descent is very steep, these "shoots" are broken up at stated intervals into long straight runs, in order to destroy the impetus which the raft would naturally acquire. The descent on one of the rafts down the timber slide is a thing only to be attempted by those who possess bold and steady nerves. To say that there is much danger in such an excursion would be to over-exaggerate the risk, whilst to say that there is none, would be as far from the truth. An application to the "boss" of a gang of raftsmen would, without difficulty, obtain the privilege of a ride down.

THE OTTAWA RIVER TO MONTREAL.

The chief lions of Ottawa being now exhausted, we will advise our tourist to prepare himself for departure for Montreal by steamboat, which starts daily, Sundays excepted, at 6.30 a.m. At this hour, and no later, the "Queen Victoria," one of the very handsome steamers of the Ottawa River Navigation Company, commanded by Captain Bowie, starts from her wharf, between the picturesque and thickly-wooded banks of the Ottawa River. Soon after leaving we obtain a fine view of the RIDEAU FALLS, which make their descent on the south side into the river. The drapery or curtainlike drop has given it its name, and gracefully and gently as it falls over, it resembles more a sheet of thin glass than a waterfall. About a mile and a-half below Ottawa, the river GATINEAU, one of the longest and most important tributaries of the Ottawa, flows into the river. Shortly after leaving Ottawa, breakfast is announced in the handsome saloon of the boat, and 18 miles off our starting point, we stop at BUCKINGHAM. THURSO, a flourishing little village, doing a large and satisfactory trade in lumber, is our next stopping point, and after two hour's more steaming, through really lovely country, and with two more stoppages at villages called BROWN'S and MAJOR'S, we reach L'ORIGNAL, and here we wish our travellers to leave the boat, for the purpose of visiting the CALEDONIA SPRINGS, nine miles off, postponing the rest of the trip to Montreal until the following day's steamer arrives, to take them on their way once again. The medecinal and healing qualities of these Springs, of which there are four in number, are very well established, and during the summer months, people flock here in large numbers to partake of the waters and to enjoy one another's society. A splendid new hotel of solid masonry, and capable of accommodating two hundred guests, has been lately erected, and we think we can offer it no higher recommendation than to say that it is now under the charge of Mr. Gianelli, of the Cosmopolitan, Montreal, who first established his reputation as "chef" to the St. James' Club of that city, and whose "Royal Italian Bitters" have since acquired a world-wide notoriety. Bowling alleys and billiard rooms have been erected, and the baths increased in number quite lately, and fitted up with every convenience.

Having rejoined our boat on the following day at L'Orignal, or proceeded in it without having made the proposed excursion to the Springs, as the case may be, we come, after seven miles, to GRENVILLE, where we have to disembark and take a twelve miles ride on the Railway cars to CARILLON. The reason for this is, that at Grenville rapids commence and continue for the distance named, and as they are not navigable for steamers, it would take up too much time for the boats to go through the Locks of the Canal. Opposite Grenville, and at the commencement of the first (Long Sault) rapids, stands HAWKESBURY, where some very large sawing mills, belonging to the Hon. John Hamilton, have been erected. It is computed that at these mills alone, 30,000,000 feet of timber are annually cut and sawn. At Carillon, we find the "Prince of Wales," (a sister ship to the one we have lately left,) under the command of Capt. Shepherd, waiting to take us on to Lachine. Before quitting this spot, we may remark that the Boundary line between the former provinces of Upper and Lower Canada, now respectively known by the names of Ontario and Quebec, leaves the centre of the river here (which had been the division for many hundred miles), and branches off in a direct line for the St. Lawrence. The banks of the river about here are high and thickly wooded, whilst its width varies between half and a quarter of a mile. On the southern shore the MOUNTAIN OF RIGAUD stands out

conspicuously against the sky, but as dinner is announced about the time we are approaching the village of the same name, we will not say much more about it for fear of spoiling the tourist's appetite, by drawing him away from the well-arranged meal waiting his digestion in the saloon. The small village of POINTE-AUX-ANGLAIS is reached at 2 p.m., HUDSON (where there are some extensive glass works), at 2.30, and COMO at 2.45, and here the river expands from about half-a-mile wide into a lake of about eight miles. This is called the LAKE OF TWO MOUNTAINS, after the two mountains to be seen on the north side rising four to five hundred feet from the water. The highest of these hills is called CALVARY, and held sacred by the tribes of the Indians inhabiting the small village of OKA, the place we see on our left hand standing at the junction between the lake and the river, and where our steamer stops for the last time before crossing the Lake to ST. ANNE'S. The Iroquois and Algonquins live in this village together, a stone wall running between the two tribes and dividing the village into two, whilst the Roman Catholic Church acts as the bond of union between them Immediately in front of us we see the ISLAND OF MONTREAL, one branch of the river passing round the Island by the right (which we follow), and the other going round to the left, and henceforth known as the Back River. Three quarters of an hour more and we are passing through the Canal and Lock at St. Anne's, in order to avoid the small rapids which run to our right under the handsome bridge belonging to, and crossed over by the Grand Trunk Railway. St. Anne's has been immortalized by Moore, in his famous Canadian Boat Song, and which is believed to have been written in the pretty little village itself. Many people know the first two lines of the chorus—Row, brothers, row, &c.,—and no more, so we fancy it will not be out of place to reproduce it here in its short entirety:—

> "Faintly as tolls the evening chime
> Our voices keep tune, and our oars keep time.
> Soon as the woods on shore look dim,
> We'll sing at St. Anne's our parting hymn.
> Row, brothers, row, the stream runs fast,
> The Rapids are near and the daylight's past.
>
> "Why should we yet our sail unfurl?
> There is not a breath the blue wave to curl;
> But when the wind blows from off the shore,
> Oh! sweetly we'll rest our weary oar.
> Blow, breezes, blow, the stream runs fast,
> The Rapids are near and the daylight's past.
>
> "Uttawas' tide! this trembling moon
> Shall see us float o'er thy surges soon.
> Saint of this green isle! hear our prayers,
> Oh, grant us cool heavens and favoring airs.
> Blow, breezes, blow, the stream runs fast,
> The Rapids are near and the daylight's past."

During the summer months St. Anne's is visited by large numbers of families from Montreal, its nearness to the city making it easy of daily access for business men, whilst the charming opportunities it offers for fishing and aquatics render it very justly sought after by the angler and amateur sailor. A mile below St. Anne's, we get into LAKE ST. LOUIS, where the Ottawa and St. Lawrence unite for the first time. As this part of our journey will also be reviewed by us when conducting our travellers from Prescott to

Montreal direct, we will simply say that the "Prince of Wales" is due to arrive at Lachine at 4.20 p.m., and that the cars of the Champlain section of the Grand Trunk Railway will be in waiting to take her passengers direct to MONTREAL, which place they will reach at 4.45 p.m., in time to make a second dinner, or supper, under the auspices of either Mr. Hogan, at the "St. Lawrence Hall," or Mr. Browning, at the newly opened Hotel, called the "Ottawa," of which establishments more hereon, at the proper time.

THE RIVER ST. LAWRENCE TO MONTREAL.

Returning to our steamer, which we left at Prescott, after discharging her travellers for Ottawa, &c., we must continue our course down the St. Lawrence to Montreal, congratulating ourselves that it has been found not only possible but perfectly safe to take these large steamers through the rapids (which commence within a few miles of Prescott), instead of necessitating the constant change from boat to stage coach, and stage coach back again to boat, as many as from five to six times between Prescott and Montreal, as our ancestors and forefathers had to do less than twenty-five years ago. WINDMILL POINT, the scene of an engagement between the American "patriots" and the British troops in 1837, is a mile below Prescott, and now in ruins. CHIMNEY ISLAND, on which are the remains of an old French fortification, is about four miles below, and the spot where the first rapids commence— THE GALLOPS. Twenty miles more, and we pass through the RAPIDE DE PLAT, and find at its foot the small village of MORRISBURG. A short distance below this we pass CHRYSLER'S FARM, a scene of a battle between the English and Americans in 1813. Farther on, we come to DICKINSON'S LANDING, seventy-seven miles from Montreal, and lying at the commencement of the LONGUE SAULT RAPIDS. This is about the most interesting and exciting portion of the route, and being the first rapids of any importance, we naturally get anxious, and wonder what be our chance amongst the foaming white waves and breakers were anything to go wrong with the boat. Once among them, we find ourselves surrounded by a turbulent and agitated mass of waters, and hurried through in a downward course by the current alone at the rate of at least twenty miles an hour, and yet, with skilful pilots, there is little or no cause for anxiety. After a few minutes of this excitement, we are pursuing the "even tenor of our way" along the river, which, but a few yards from the foot of the rapids, flows on with an almost unruffled surface. A continuous line of islands divides the waters of the St. Lawrence almost entirely down the extent of the Longue Sault Rapids, and at their foot these two currents unite and dash into one another at a place called the "Big Pitch." CORNWALL is situated, on the Canadian shore, at the foot of these rapids, and nearly opposite, partly on American and partly on British soil, a remnant of the once powerful tribe of the Iroquois Indians, now inhabit the picturesque village of St. Regis. The men here chiefly subsist on what they can get by hunting or shooting, whilst the females of the tribe make a small competency out of the sale of ornamental bead-work and moccasins, and the manufacture of brooms and baskets. There is a large stone Roman Catholic Church in the village, built nearly 150 years ago, containing two handsome bells in its belfry. Henceforth the two shores of the St. Lawrence belong to the Canadian Dominion, the boundary between the States and Canada leaves the river here, and strikes across inland in a direct or air line. A short distance below this spot the river expands into a lake of about five miles broad and forty miles long, called Lake St. Francis. LANCASTER is situated on the northern shore, in about the centre, and a small village called COTEAU DU LAC is at the termination of the Lake, and immediately below are the COTEAU RAPIDS, followed at short intervals by the CEDARS and CASCADE RAPIDS. The village of BEAUHARNOIS is situated at the foot of the Cascades, and twenty-seven miles from Montreal. There is a canal of eleven miles in length here, in order for vessels ascending the river, to avoid these rapids,—indeed, by the side of every one of these rapids there are canals, as it would be, of course, impossible for any vessel, steam or not, to make head against the mass of descending waters, and without them the river would not virtually be navigable. Almost immediately afterwards, the St. Lawrence expands once more into a lake, which is called Lake St. Louis. It is into the northern portion of this Lake that the waters of the Ottawa flow, though from each stream maintaining its own natural colour, it is not until the Lachine Rapids are gained that they appear to unite. Five miles below Beauharnois we pass NUN'S ISLAND, cultivated by and belonging to the Grey Nunnery, Montreal. A mile from this the Chateauguay River discharges itself into the Lake, and within a few minutes we pass abreast of LACHINE (a favorite watering place in the summer months for Montreal families) on the northern side, and CAUGHNAWAGA, an Indian village, on the southern side. The current here commences to run very quickly, and before many moments are passed we shall find ourselves entering the broken waters at the head of the LACHINE RAPIDS. A retrograde motion is, of course, impossible here, and "onwards" must, perforce, be our motto. We are now "taking the Rapids" for the last time, and perhaps, of all that we have passed, these are the most exciting, as at the very moment when you feel you are making direct for a ledge of rock, and cannot possibly avoid striking, you find the helm suddenly turned by the united power of four men, and you have passed the impending danger, and are once more safely steaming down the calm, placid stream below the Rapids. No one should come to Montreal without "shooting the Rapids," and to those who reach it by train, or from the Ottawa River, it is quite easy for them to enjoy the excitement; for every morning at 7 o'clock a train leaves Bonaventure Station for Lachine, connecting with the beautiful little steamer

"Aurora," which starts from the Railway Wharf as soon as she has her freight of travellers, shoots the rapids, passes under the Victoria Bridge, and lands her passengers again in Montreal by nine in the morning, with an appetite for breakfast much heightened by their early excursion. But to return to our steamer. After having run the rapids, we pass the village of LA PRAIRIE, and immediately come in sight of the city of Montreal, commercially and actually the most important place in British North America, and destined some day, perchance, to rival the population and the prosperity of some of the overgrown cities of the Old World.

Before reaching the wharf, we pass under the centre span of the eighth wonder of the world—the VICTORIA BRIDGE of the GRAND TRUNK RAILWAY OF CANADA.

MONTREAL.

Montreal was founded in the year 1642, nearly on the site of the old Indian settlement, called Hochelaga, and the name "Ville Marie" was given to the city. Afterwards the name was changed to Mount Royal, from the mountain standing at the back of the city, and this name has since been corrupted into Montreal.

Within the last twenty or thirty years the city has made many steps towards material improvement. Quays, running from two to three miles, have been built along the banks of the river, and public and private edifices of cut-stone have been erected throughout the whole city. Following the rule of most other large towns, the chief building operations have been carried on westwards, and spots that a few years back were nothing but fields, are now occupied by handsomely built terraces, or elegant villas, belonging to the merchant princes of Montreal; from the rapid strides made in this direction, it is difficult to say where this advance will stop.

The inhabitants of Montreal are composed of a number of different nationalities,—the French Canadians and the Irish predominating in numbers, consequently the Roman Catholic religion may be considered numerically to be the prevailing creed in the city. The Protestant faith, on the other hand, as far as wealth and influence are concerned, shows no symptoms of losing ground. Montreal is the See for both a Roman Catholic and Church of England Bishoprick, the latter being the Metropolitan of all the Dominion of Canada. It is also the largest garrisoned city in British North America, there being as many as five regiments quartered there, with two batteries of Artillery, and some Engineers. The Commander of the Forces, surrounded by a large Staff, resides there. The Volunteers are very numerous also, and a very large Drill Shed is now being built for them, at the expense of the Corporation. Though very little fortified externally, the city is well protected against invasion. During the summer months, the troops in garrison parade every day on the "Champ de Mars," and the numerous military bands play in one or other of the public gardens two or three times a week, making the place very lively for any visitors who may chance to be in the neighbourhood.

We shall endeavor, in their order, to describe some of the principal public buildings in the city, which, besides being very numerous, are architecturally superior to those of almost any other city on the Continent. At first, we shall house our tourist at one or other of the two principal hotels in the city. The " St. Lawrence Hall" being the largest and best known, is entitled to the first word of praise. It has been under the skilful management of Mr. Hogan, the proprietor, for the last seventeen years, and gradually been gaining in public favor every succeeding year. It is capable of putting up 500 visitors, and during the months of travel, this accommodation is nightly required; so much so, that visitors are frequently unable to obtain rooms. The other hotel is the " Ottawa," situated, like the " Hall," in Great St. James Street, the principal thoroughfare of the city. This house was closed during the winters of 1867–68, while it underwent very extensive alterations, additions and repairs. It is now reopened, under the charge of its former proprietor, Mr. Browning, and capable of accommodating over 300 guests. The rooms have been refurnished, and the house will, we feel assured, receive increased reputation and the patronage its spirited owner so richly merits.

The Cathedrals and Churches of Montreal are, of course, among its chief attractions. The Roman Catholic Cathedral occupies one side of the French Square, or Place d'Armes, in the very centre of the city. It is supposed to be the largest building in America, and can contain 10,000 people without undue crowding. It is built of Montreal stone, in the perpendicular Gothic style of the middle ages, with twin Gothic towers. The view *of* these can be seen for miles distant, and the view *from* these is necessarily most extensive. Christ Church Cathedral (C. of E.) is at the corner of Union Avenue and St. Catherine Street, in the upper part of the town; a beautiful edifice, built partly of Montreal and partly of Caen (Normandy) stone, in the Mediæval-Gothic style. The principal entrance is very handsome indeed, and the Cathedral should be visited by all tourists, as many say that there is not another building like it on the continent. Numerous other churches are distributed all over the city. Our space is too confined, unfortunately, to mention more, suffice it to say that almost every creed—nay, sect—has some place of worship in Montreal.

The Court House is a commanding pile in cut-stone, in the Grecian-Ionic style, and contains Court Rooms for the Superior, Criminal, Circuit and Appeal Cases, besides a spacious Legal Library and offices in connection with the different Courts. It is situated between Notre Dame Street and the Champ de Mars. Bonsecours Market next claims our notice, standing on the quay, surmounted by a large dome, which is visible all over the city, and is an example of the Grecian-Doric style of architecture. A dead meat market extends nearly the whole length of the building, on the ground floor; whilst in the basement, fish and vegetables are offered for sale. A

1. Quebec Custom House.
2. Montreal Bank.

large Concert Room, and Common Council Chambers, occupy the whole of the first flat. McGill College is situated a little back from Sherbrooke Street, in the upper part of the city, and immediately in front of the Reservoir. It contains Lecture and Class Rooms, and a large Library, and is the home for Schools of Medicine, Arts and Law. It was founded by the late Hon. James McGill, and a new wing, called the "Molson Wing," has lately been added, at the expense of Wm. Molson, Esq. St. Patrick's Hall, in Victoria Square, has been lately finished. It stands alone, and contains one of the finest halls in America, extending the entire length and breadth of the building on the upper floor, 134 feet by 94 feet, and 46 feet high. The lower stories are devoted to Library, Committee Rooms, a Billiard Hall, and stores. It is built of Montreal limestone, the style of architecture being an adaptation of the Norman. The Albert Buildings, in Victoria Square, and the Dominion Block, in McGill Street, are quite lately erected, in the best style possible for wholesale stores and offices, and are most imposing buildings, quite surpassing anything previously attempted in the Dominion.

The Bank buildings, perhaps, demand our next attention. The Bank of Montreal faces the French Cathedral in Place d'Armes, with six massive stone columns as a portico. A very handsome stone-sculptured pediment has lately been added to the façade surmounting the Corinthian columns. Molsons Bank, in Great St. James Street, is a very handsome building, in Ohio sandstone, with granite columns, the whole front of the edifice being finely decorated with stone carvings. The Bank of Ontario, on the west side of Place d'Armes, is built in the Italian style of architecture, and very justly admired. Several of the other banks in the city have also very handsome buildings wherein to transact their increasing business.

There are very many charitable institutions in Montreal, of which the principal are the Hôtel Dieu, the English General Hospital, the Protestant House of Industry and Refuge, *cum multis aliis* too numerous to name.

Insurance Offices, Clubs, and Wholesale and Retail Stores, all have conspicuous and handsome edifices to boast of, and several days can be most satisfactorily devoted to seeing some or all of these buildings, and to taking a drive or two in the neighbourhood, especially " Round the Mountain," which is about nine miles in circumference. A few drives of this sort will give a better idea of the wealth and prosperity of the city, and of its daily growing importance, than the description of the place extended over a hundred pages of a Guide. The Victoria Bridge should be inspected, which can be done by driving to Point St. Charles, and obtaining an order from the Grand Trunk Railway authorities, whose General Offices are situated quite close to the northern end of the abutment. It is one of the most stupendous engineering achievements of the present day, when the rapidity of the current and the length of the structure are taken into consideration. The bridge is on the tubular system, consisting of 23 spans of 242 feet each, with a centre span of 330 feet, and is just two miles long. It was opened by H. R. H. the Prince of Wales, in August, 1860, and connects the Eastern District of the Grand Trunk Railway with Montreal and the West. Of the importance of such a national undertaking it is needless to speak.

In 1860, Montreal numbered 90,000 inhabitants. In the present year, the number is somewhat over 130,000, and rapidly increasing by about 10,000 annually.

In the summer months, the magnificent fleet of vessels belonging to the Montreal Ocean Steamship Company, owned by Messrs. H. & A. Allan, come right up to Montreal, from Liverpool, and embark and disembark all their freight at one of the quays. During this season, the river is alive with vessels of every conceivable tonnage, and the scene from the banks is most lively. From Montreal, we propose to take our travellers down the river to Quebec, and, as we have now mentioned the chief points to be seen in this interesting city, we will prepare for our departure. The Richelieu Company own two splendid vessels, the "Montreal," and the "Quebec," which make the trip between Montreal and Quebec every night, except Sunday, during the time that navigation is open. Any traveller preferring the land route, can take the trains leaving Bonaventure Station on the Grand Trunk Railway, and, after an eight hours' journey, be deposited at Point Levi, opposite "the Ancient Capital," as Quebecers are fond of styling their city, whence a steam ferry will soon land them across the river. To our mind, however, the most agreeable route is to go on board the "Quebec," take a state-room, and be landed early next morning at one of the quays of Quebec. Leaving, therefore, Montreal at about six any evening, on the arrival of the steamer from Upper Canada, we steam out between St. Helen's Island (a strongly fortified place, inhabited only by the military) and the Island of Montreal, and, after passing Sorel, Lake St. Peter, and Three Rivers, we are awoke in the morning by the stoppage of the paddles, and find ourselves along the wharf at Quebec.

QUEBEC.

As soon as the traveller is landed, we recommend him to make his way as quickly as possible to either the "St. Louis Hotel" or "Russell House," both of which establishments are kept by Messrs. Russell & Sons, who honestly deserve to be classed amongst the most enterprising hotel proprietors on the American Continent. At either of these houses the tourist will find himself at home and well cared for, surrounded by every comfort he can possibly desire. The "St. Louis" has recently been very much enlarged and improved, to meet the increasing requirements of the American travel, and too much credit cannot be awarded to the Messrs. Russell, who are ever ready to embark their means for the purpose of inducing their friends from the States to pay the old Capital a visit. Every modern convenience and luxury is to be found in these hotels, and we are quite satisfied that the experience of any who may visit Quebec will be like our own, and lead to oft repeated journeys to the old city. Quebec, formerly the capital of United Canada, is situated on the north shore of the St. Lawrence. It was founded by Charlevoix, in 1608, on the site of an Indian village called Stadacona. It has a population of about 50,000. It is divided into two parts, known as the Upper and Lower Towns. The Upper Town is well fortified, ranking in point of strength next to Gibraltar : the Citadel of Cape Diamond being well known as the most formidable fortress in America. The suburbs of St. Roch and St. John extend along the River St. Charles to the Plains of Abraham. Quebec was taken by the British and Colonial forces in 1629, but restored to France in 1632; and was finally captured by Wolfe in 1759, and, with all the French possessions in North America, was ceded to Great Britain at the peace of 1763.

The city and the suburbs contain 174 streets, among the principal of which are the following :— St John Street, occupied by retail stores ; St. Louis Street, by lawyers offices and private dwellings ; D'Auteuil Street faces the Esplanade, and is occupied by private residences ; Grande Allée, or St. Louis Road, outside St. Louis Gate, and leading to the Plains of Abraham, is a beautiful street, and contains many elegant villa residences. The principal street in the Lower Town is St. Peter, and contains alike with all the other streets, banks, merchants' and insurance offices. The principal buildings are the Custom House, the Marine Hospital, the Parliament

Buildings, and the different Gates, which were formerly the only entrances to the city.

By applying at the offices of the hotels, every possible information can be ascertained as to the most desirable places to visit in and around Quebec, and the best means of doing so according to the time at the command of the guests, and carriages can be ordered with drivers capable of giving those desiring it a thorough acquaintance with the place and its associations. We enumerate the following, which should all be visited, if the time of our reader will admit. SPENCER WOOD, the late residence of the Governor-General, is a nice easy distance from the city, and the view from it is very fine indeed. The PLAINS OF ABRAHAM are celebrated in history as being the death scene of Generals Wolfe and Montcalm. The battle ground presents almost a level surface from the bank of the St. Lawrence to the St. Foy Road. On the highest ground, considerably in advance of the Martello Towers, not far from the fence which divides the Race Grounds from the enclosures on the east, are the remains of a Redoubt, close by which a rock is pointed out as marking the spot where Wolfe actually breathed his last. Montcalm, who survived him but a few hours, was buried in an excavation made by the bursting of a shell within the precincts of the Ursuline Convent. His skull was exhumed some 12 years ago, and placed in a glass case in the convent, where those who are desirous can see it on application to the Chaplain there. THE FALLS OF MONTMORENCI are about seven miles down the river, and, when seen, will amply compensate for any time or trouble in driving there. The Montmorenci Stream, so called after a French Admiral of that name, is small, but the Falls are quite worthy of their very high reputation, and no visitor to Quebec should leave without having a sight of them. The Falls are about 250 feet, rushing over the precipice in an unbroken mass, discharging themselves into a pool below which boils and foams as if venting its wrath at having been tossed about, till in a few moments the water glides onward in peace, to mingle with the current of the St. Lawrence. The Falls being only fifty feet in width, when compared with the height causes the latter to seem greater than it really is. In winter, the Falls are a great attraction as well to Quebecers as to those who have an opportunity of visiting the city. The foam and spray rising from the foot of the Falls accumulate in the shape of ice, forming a cone oftentimes reaching to a height of nearly 100 feet. A smaller one, called "The Ladies' Cone," is also found at its side, and these are made use of for tobogganing—that is, parties having ascended to the summit, entrust themselves to their hand-sleigh or "toboggan," and slide down at full speed, gaining velocity every instant, and are carried sometimes half a mile or more on the surrounding level ice. There are men and boys in attendance for the purpose of bringing down strangers who may desire to venture down the icy mountain, and to those who enjoy this kind of pleasure, it is great sport. The drive to the Falls is very beautiful; the scenery on the road through BEAUPORT, where the Provincial Lunatic Asylum is built, and back again being full of interest. About two miles above the Falls is a curious formation on the river bank, called THE NATURAL STEPS, a series of layers of the limestone rock, each about a foot in thickness, and for about half-a-mile receding one above the other, to the height of nearly 20 feet, as regularly as if formed by the hand of man. They are a great object of wonder and curiosity, and, being so near the Falls, should certainly be included in the visit. LORETTE is an Indian Village, situated about nine miles from the city, which, next to the Falls, should be seen. In the place itself, there is perhaps nothing very important, but the drive is one which cannot fail to please, and the Indians are well deserving of a visit. All kinds of fancy basket work, etc., executed by "the Squaws," may be purchased at this village, at extremely low prices, and are alike useful and ornamental.

A very nice drive will be found in going out to CAPE ROUGE, commonly known as CAROUGE. It is like all the drives in and around Quebec, very pretty, and cannot fail to give enjoyment to those fond of good roads and interesting scenery. We would strongly recommend this place to be visited by all going to Quebec, who can possibly afford the time after seeing what we have previously enumerated.

We feel sure our reader, whatever his pretensions may be as a traveller, will be delighted with the ancient city of Quebec, and have a satisfactory feeling of pleasure within himself for having included it in the catalogue of places he has put down as worthy of a visit in his tour

1 Quebec from Point Levi.
2 Montmorenci Falls, near Quebec.

through Canada. The scenery outside the city, and all along the river on both shores, is exceedingly picturesque, every yard bringing a new and varied landscape into view, calculated to please the imagination, delight the eye, and satisfy the most fastidious in natural beauty.

We find the following in Buckingham's Canada: " The situation of Quebec is highly advantage-
" ous in a commercial as well as military point
" of view; and its appearance is very imposing
" from whatever quarter it is first approached.
" Though at a distance of 400 miles from the sea,
" the magnificent river on which it is seated is
" three miles in breadth a little below the town,
" and narrows into about a mile in breadth im-
" mediately abreast of the Citadel, having in both
" these parts sufficient depth of water for the
" largest ships in the world—a rise and fall of
" twenty feet in its tides—and space enough in
" its capacious basin, between Cape Diamond on
" the one hand, and the Isle of Orleans on the
" other, to afford room and anchorage for a
" thousand sail of vessels at a time, sheltered
" from all winds, and perfectly secure."

The RIVER CHAUDIERE is about nine miles below Quebec, and THE FALLS are very beautiful. The leap is over a precipice, 130 feet in height —the width of the Fall being nearly 40 feet.

THE LOWER ST. LAWRENCE RIVER.

Leaving Quebec, we advise the tourist to at once make his arrangements for visiting that very popular resort, THE SAGUENAY. For the past few years, thousands of Canadians and Americans have wended their way to this famous River, and the result of their experience has been to make it still more popular. None who have been here have resolved otherwise than to repeat the trip the first time they could possibly do so, and to those who have not enjoyed this most lovely of all excursions, we would say, in the language of Shakspeare, "stand not upon the order of your going, but go at once." All information concerning the means of transit can be ascertained at the hotels to which we took our *compagnons de voyage;* but in case they may neglect to attend to the important duty of seeking such requisite knowledge, we would say that in the early part of the season the steamer "Union," and afterwards the steamer "Magnet," make the trip from Quebec to the Saguenay. Both these boats belong to the Canadian Navigation Company, whose steamers ply between Hamilton, Toronto and Montreal. They are elegantly fitted up for the comfort of passengers, and furnished with every convenience; indeed, there is nothing wanting to render the journey down the river what it always is, most delightful. Captain Simpson, who is in command of the "Magnet," has been on this route in the Canadian Navigation Company's service for many years, and will, doubtless, be well known to many already. To those unacquainted with him, we can only say, take your quarters on board the "Magnet" if possible, and make his acquaintance immediately, and we can vouch for the trip to the Saguenay being a very jolly and pleasant one. Once on board and off, we find ourselves steaming away down stream at a good speed, and to turn our thoughts away from the city we have just left, we find coming into view the ISLAND OF ORLEANS, which lies just below Quebec. It is nineteen miles in length by five and a-half miles in width, and has a population of over 5,000. The FALLS OF ST. ANNE are at the confluence of the River St. Anne with the St. Lawrence, 24 miles below Quebec. The surrounding scenery is both wild and beautiful. LAKE ST. CHARLES, thirteen miles north of Quebec, is celebrated for its fine trout, and is a very desirable resort for anglers. MURRAY BAY is the first stopping place for the steamer after leaving Quebec, and where many may desire to go ashore and spend a day or two before going further. Murray Bay is a great resort in the summer months, and many Canadian families spend the entire season in this healthy retreat. Every one must enjoy a few days passed at this fashionable watering place. Leaving Murray Bay and steaming across the river, which is about 20 miles wide at this point, we strike RIVIÈRE DU LOUP, situated on the south shore. Here those desirous of visiting the far-famed watering-place of CACOUNA land, and, after an exceedingly pleasant drive through the country of about 6 miles, find themselves in a fashionable place, containing some very good buildings. The "St. Lawrence Hall," where we would strongly advise the visitor to make for, is a large house, replete with every modern convenience and comfort; every accommodation to be obtained at any of our first city hotels can be found here, together with a good

Billiard Room, Bowling Alley, and hot and cold baths; sea-bathing is provided for in connection with the hotel, and sailing boats are kept ready for the use of visitors desirous of going out on the river on fishing and shooting excursions. A week spent with "mine host" at the St. Lawrence will always be looked back to with pleasure.

Leaving the wharf at Rivière du Loup, our steamer points her course again to the opposite shore and in less than two hours we find ourselves at TADOUSAC, which is at the mouth of the RIVER SAGUENAY. This is a very pleasant spot, and, if no more time can be spared than the brief stay of the steamboat at the wharf, let us advise the tourist to immediately go ashore. There is a fine hotel here, which is excellently kept, and in connection with it are all kinds of sports for the amusement of visitors. The bathing at this place is also very superior.

Getting aboard again, the whistle is sounded, and we are again under steam, and are really now entering the justly-renowned RIVER SAGUENAY, and commence, as if by instinct, to strain our eyes and open our mouths, to feast on and swallow all the magnificent natural grandeur that bursts upon us.

THE SAGUENAY RIVER.

The Saguenay is the largest tributary of the great St. Lawrence, and unquestionably one of the most remarkable rivers on the Continent. It is the principal outlet of Lake St. John, which is its head-water: a lake about forty miles long, surrounded by a heavily timbered and level country; its waters are remarkably clear, and abound in a great variety of fine fish. Eleven large rivers fall into it, yet it has only this one outlet; into the lake there is a remarkable curtain Fall of two hundred and thirty-six feet, so conspicuous as to be seen at forty or fifty miles distant, the Indian name for which is "Oueat Chouan" or "Do you see a fall there?" The Lake lies about 150 miles north-east of the St. Lawrence, and nearly due north of Quebec. The original name of the Saguenay was Chicoutimi, signifying "Deep water"; but the early Jesuit missionaries gave it the name it now bears, said to be a corruption of St. Jean Nez. The scenery is wild and romantic in the highest degree. The first half of its course averages half-a-mile in width and runs through an almost untrodden wilderness; it abounds in falls and rapids, and is only navigable for the Indian canoe. A few miles below the southern fall in the river is the village of Chicoutimi, at the junction of a river of the same name, which is the outlet of a long lake named Kenokami, with the Saguenay. Here is a range of rapids which extend ten miles. The Indians say there is a subterranean Fall above the foot of the rapids, which they call "Manitou," or the "Great Spirit." To avoid these falls, there is a carrying place called "LE GRANDE PORTAGE." An extensive lumber business is transacted here; the village has an ancient appearance, and contains about five hundred inhabitants. The only curiosity is a rude Catholic Church, said to have been one of the earliest founded by the Jesuits. It occupies the centre of a grassy lawn, surrounded by shrubbery, backed by a cluster of wood-crowned hills, and commands a fine prospect, not only of the Saguenay, but also of the spacious bay formed by the confluence of the two rivers. In the belfry of this venerable church hangs a clear-toned bell, with an inscription upon it which has never yet been translated or expounded. From ten to twelve miles south of Chicoutimi, a beautiful expanse of water, called GRAND or HA! HA! BAY, recedes from the Saguenay, to the distance of several miles.

The village of Grand Bay, 132 miles from Quebec, is the usual resort for those who wish to remain any time in the neighbourhood of the Saguenay. The name Ha! Ha! is said to be derived from the surprise which the French experienced when they first entered it, supposing it to be still the river, until their shallop grounded on the north-western shore. At the northern head of it is another settlement, called BAGGOTVILLE. Between these two places the Saguenay is rather shallow (when compared with the remainder of its course) and varies in width from two and a half to three miles. The tide is observable as far north as Chicoutimi, and this entire section of the river is navigable for ships of the largest class, which ascend thus far for lumber.

That portion of the Saguenay extending from Ha! Ha! Bay to the St. Lawrence, a distance of nearly sixty miles, is chiefly distinguished, and properly so, for its wonderful scenery. The shores are composed principally of granite, and every bend presents to view an imposing bluff—many of these tower perpendicularly into the air, and seem ready to totter and fall at any moment—it appears awful, in steaming up the Saguenay, to raise the eyes heavenward and behold, hanging directly over head, a mass of granite weighing, perhaps, nearly a million tons. Here, as at Niagara, we feel the insignificance of man as we gaze upon the Almighty's handiworks.

Descending from Ha! Ha! Bay, a perpendicular rock, nine hundred feet high, is the abrupt termination of a lofty plateau called THE TABLEAU, a column of dark-colored granite, 600 feet high by 300 wide, with its sides as smooth as if they had received the polishing stroke from a sculptor's chisel. STATUE POINT is also another gem of scenery; but the great attractions in the Saguenay are CAPE ETERNITY AND TRINITY POINT, on the south shore, six miles above St. John's Bay. If the only recompense for a visit to the Saguenay was a sight of these stupendous promontories, we are quite sure no visitor would ever regret it. There is an awful grandeur and sublimity about them, which is perfectly indescribable. The steamers shut off steam at these points and the best view possible is arranged for the passengers by the Captain. The water is said to be as deep five feet from their base as it is in the centre of the stream, and, from actual measurement, many portions of it have been ascertained to be a thousand feet, and the shallowest parts not less than a hundred; and from the overhanging cliffs it assumes a black and ink-like appearance. Cape

Eternity is by far the most imposing, and an Indian hunter, having followed a Moose to the brow of the cliff after the deer had made a fatal spring far down into the deep water, is said to have lost his foothold and perished with his prey. We also learn from "LeMoine's Oiseaux du Canada," that two or three years ago two fine specimens of the bird of Washington, that rare eagle, were shot here; and indeed continually the flight of the bald-headed eagles along the summits of these beetling cliffs—the salmon leaping after its insect prey—or the seals bobbing their heads out of the water, attract the sportsman's eye.

Nothing can surpass the magnificent salmon fishing of the MARGUERITE, and other streams, tributaries to the Saguenay, and full particulars with regard to these matters can be obtained at the hotels before leaving Quebec.

Before taking our departure from what must certainly be classed as one of the most lovely and picturesque spots in North America, we would pause to ask the tourist whether his expectations have not been fully realized in every respect, and even far exceeded. We feel satisfied an affirmative answer is the only one that can be given to such a question, for there can be no two opinions as to the magnificence of the scenery brought before the vision on a trip up the River Saguenay to Ha! Ha! Bay.

Leaving Tadousac then, on the return journey, the steamer again makes its way across the St. Lawrence to Rivière du Loup, for the convenience of Cacouna passengers, and those desirous, by so arranging it, can here go ashore, and

1. L'Anse a L'Eau, Saguenay.
2. Tadousac and Mouth of Saguenay River.

take the train by the Grand Trunk Railway to Quebec. Having sailed down the river, this will prove an interesting change, and bring them into Quebec much earlier. Those remaining on the boat will, if a fine day, enjoy the sail, calling at Murray Bay (Malbaie), as on the downward trip, and afterwards making straight for Quebec. Those tourists taking the train at Rivière du Loup can make connection at Point Levi, which is opposite Quebec, with trains for the White Mountains, the next place at which we purpose stopping with them. Those who still keep to the boat, on arrival at Quebec will probably prefer lying over a day for rest before proceeding on their journey.

From POINT LEVI there is not much to be seen, and we therefore advise our traveller as soon as possible to get a sleeping berth in the train, have a good night's rest, and be in good trim on reaching the White Mountains. At RICHMOND STATION, which is the junction with the main line of the Grand Trunk Railway, our tourist can have a comfortable meal at the Station and then change cars, getting on board the train *from* Montreal, which also has a sleeping car attached to it, the train he has travelled by from Quebec being the mail train *for* Montreal.

THE WHITE MOUNTAINS.

A few hours after this he will find himself, after a very pretty ride through a mountainous country, at GORHAM, and, on landing, will be almost within arm's length of the door of the " Alpine House," a very fine hotel, where he will do well to get himself ensconced as quickly as possible. The worthy host, Mr. J. R. Hitchcock, will be on hand with his smiling countenance ready to make the traveller happy and comfortable after his weary journey. From this house, places of interest all about the mountains are within easy distance, and carriages and saddle-horses in great numbers are kept on hand for visiting the various beautiful spots in and around Gorham. There are numerous drives, which are all exceedingly pretty, and indeed the WHITE MOUNTAINS is destined to become one of the most fashionable resorts on this continent.

" The White Mountains, or the Switzerland of
" America, are situated in Coos County, New
" Hampshire, and consist of a number of moun-
" tain peaks, from four to six thousand feet in
" altitude, the highest of them being Mount
" Washington, which is six thousand two hundred
" and forty-three feet above the level of the sea,
" and possesses the greatest attraction to tourists.
" Its ascent has lately become quite fashionable
" with visitors to the mountains. It is perhaps
" impossible to find anything grander in moun-
" tain scenery than the White Mountains of New
" Hampshire. From the 'Alpine House' visit-
" ors can proceed by carriages eight miles to the
" 'Glen House,' which is at the base of Mount
" Washington, and there take saddle-horses for
" the ascent. The 'Notch' is a narrow gorge
" between two enormous cliffs, and extends for a
" distance of two miles. Its entrance is nearly

" twenty feet wide, and the mountain scenery
" diversified by beautiful cascades falling over
" perpendicular rocks, is grand in the extreme.
" The 'Willey House' stands in this nitch, at an
" elevation of two thousand feet. It is pointed
" out to the traveller as the residence of the
" Willey family, who perished by an avalanche
" from the mountain thirty years ago. In Fran-
" cania Nitch may be seen the Basin and Flume,
" objects of great interest. The Flume is a
" stream of water having a fall of two hundred
" and fifty feet over fearful precipices into a natu-
" ral cavity in the rocks, which forms the basin.
" The 'Old Man of the Mountain,' or profile
" mountain, is a singularly interesting natural
" object. It obtains its name from the striking
" resemblance it bears to the profile of the human
" countenance, every feature being marked with
" the greatest accuracy."

Travellers should arrange their plans so as to spend a portion of their time on the mountains, which they can accomplish by taking up their quarters at the " Glen House." This fine Hotel, well known to tourists, has all the comforts of the first class city houses, and being beautifully and conveniently situated, is a most desirable residence for all who intend "doing" the mountains scramble.

Leaving the White Mountains, and the hospitalities of the Alpine House, we take our seat in the train at Gorham Station for Portland, and find ourselves whizzing along through a magnificent mountainous country, which probably excels anything of its kind in America, and we would recommend a good look out being kept during the journey, for the varied scenery cannot fail to please. On arrival at SOUTH PARIS, those desirous have time to obtain refreshments, and those who are accustomed to travel well know that it is just as well to take good care of the inner man, so as to be securely fortified against the fatigue that always, more or less, attends long journies.

PORTLAND.

After leaving South Paris, nothing of note is seen until a short distance off Portland, when we come in sight of the Atlantic, and feel that sense of pleasure which is experienced on getting near home after a long absence. Arrived at PORTLAND, the principal city of Maine, our tourist will feel that, if not virtually at home, he is at least in its neighbourhood, and among friends. To those who have never been in Portland, and can spare the necessary time, we would say, spend a day or two there by all means. It is one of the most pleasant and agreeable cities in the Eastern States, with wide streets and avenues nicely kept, well meriting its title, "The Forest City." CAPE ELIZABETH is a very favorite resort, and being but a few miles out of the city, an afternoon cannot be better passed than by taking a drive out there. Excursions can also be made to the "Ocean House" and "Orchard Beach," both of which are exceedingly pleasant. Then there are the 365 Islands, most of which can be reached by ferry-boat or yacht, and where there are always to be found a great many visitors seeking health and relaxation from business. At several of these Islands first-class hotels are to be found, and every comfort can be obtained.

In Portland, the "Falmouth Hotel," kept by Messrs. Ramsay and Wheeler, is an exceedingly fine house and very handsomely furnished. The "Preble House" and "United States Hotel" are both very well kept, equipped with every comfort, and are very desirable houses in every respect. The "St. Julien," which is kept on the "European plan," will also be found a very nice house, well kept, and furnished with every accommodation and convenience for the comfort of its guests.

From Portland, two or three different routes can be chosen, according to the time and inclination of the traveller. If desiring to get to New York direct, and preferring a sea passage, steamers ply regularly, and in fine weather this will be found an exceedingly pleasant trip. We shall, however, presume that the majority travelling intend to go *viâ* Boston, and, if possible, rest a while in that fine city, rather than hurry on at railroad speed, which cannot but prove tiresome. Therefore, to such there is the choice of land or water carriage. Steamers, elegantly furnished, of thorough sea-going qualities, leave Portland every evening for Boston, the passage occupying about ten hours, and, if adopting this mode of conveyance, passengers are landed after a complete night's rest, free from the weariness attending a journey by railway. Those preferring the road, can take the train in the morning, afternoon or evening, there being three daily, occupying five hours on the journey

BOSTON.

Arriving in BOSTON, we have again got back into the midst of business and excitement, and we see more life than we have witnessed since we sallied forth in our wanderings from New York. Our traveller will doubtless desire to get comfortably quartered during his sojourn here, if only for a brief period, and to do this he has only need to make his way to the "Revere House," or the "Tremont," both first-class hotels, where every comfort and luxury is to be met with. There are many things to be visited in and around Boston, but as doubtless our readers will be well acquainted with the city and its surroundings, it is needless to recount all the various places of interest which have been so frequently and lucidly described; albeit we cannot pass hence without advising all those who have never visited MOUNT AUBURN, to do so ere they return home. The Cemetery is indeed a lovely spot, and a few hours is delightfully spent in walking or driving through its beautiful grounds. Here is seen the handiwork too of many a fond heart towards their departed loved ones, and the taste displayed generally has tended to make the place very charming. Harvard University, which is situated at CAMBRIDGE, about four miles from Boston, should also be visited. It is here that Longfellow lives, among other American celebrities who have settled down within the shade of their former "Alma Mater." The large Organ, in the

Boston Music Hall, is visited by great numbers, and performances are given twice a week. If the tourist should be fortunate enough to be in Boston on either day this takes place, he will do well to make a point of attending and enjoying what is a rare treat to all lovers of good music. Information can be obtained at the hotels as to the days and time, and tickets for admission can also be procured.

Leaving Boston, we will now make our way homewards to New York, and deposit the tourist at the place from which we started with him, and in doing this we will again leave him to his choice of routes, as there are several; but, if our opinion be of any use, we would strongly advise him to take the train to Newport, and thence go by one of the magnificent steamers running from that place. This is a lovely trip, and the boats are comfortable in all their appointments, and in ten to twelve hours he will be landed safely in the great city—

NEW YORK.

Here we are again at New York. But before losing ourselves among its 1,200,000 inhabitants we raise our hat to the departing reader with the hope that the trip here ended has been a pleasant one. "On different senses, different objects strike;" but we think there has been something of a sort to please all. Men of every pursuit, and of every variety of taste, will have been able to indulge, each in his peculiar hobby; for although the extent of ground traversed may not seem so large as otherwise might appear, from the similarity of race everywhere encountered, yet, from the free expression given to thought, and the amount of enterprise, social and individual, everywhere met with, there is perhaps not a better field open for examining the working merits of the different schemes which have been from time to time proposed, as affording solutions of the important questions of national education, workmen's associations, co-operative labour, &c., &c.

To the political economist there has been, therefore, abundant subject for fruitful study; and the prospects of an ever-increasing wealth, lately opened by the discovery of rich mineral veins in territory hitherto regarded as unproductive, will afford the theorist grounds on which to work, in conducting his speculations on the great future reserved for this continent.

To the geologist, no tract of country would well be found more replete with interest than that we have traversed. He has been brought face to face with nature in her sublimest aspects; he has been admitted, as it were, to view the *arcana* of her great workshop, and the vast cutting scooped out by the degrading force exerted through successive ages on a limestone formation by a stupendous power like Niagara, to the tiny "striæ" or ice grooves, that to this day mark with unerring line the course of the Northern glaciers, as in ages still more remote they ground down over the greater portion of the North American area.

The artist and sportsman have also no reason

to complain of the bill of fare offered for their especial enjoyment. The former could hardly study in a better school than that he has just left—a school that has produced more than one conscientious interpreter of its own peculiar "*genre;*" and of late years none more entitled to our hearty approval than M. Jacobi. And the latter will on his journey round have been able to inspect, in the larger cities, the spoils of many a game bag and fishing basket. We have not in our leaves touched much on this topic, but can recommend any of our readers to purchase and be guided by the information which can be obtained in the pages of "The Canadian Handbook and Tourist's Guide," edited by J. Taylor, and published in Montreal.

The student of life and character will have occasion to notice many novelties; and the strange mixture of the two languages in Canada, by the "*habitants,*" as they are called, will astonish his ideas of euphony. His pure French, if such, perchance, he can command, will not unfrequently prove "*caviare*" to these swarthy folks; but, perhaps, nothing will have more effect on him than the first sight obtained of the red-man, such as he appears in the streets of our cities in this the 19th century. "*O quantum mutatus ab illo*" he will exclaim—from that romantic-looking creature clothed in a scanty allowance of "fig-leaf," who used to be served up for the delectation of our infantile minds in the pages of Old Peter Parley—when he sees the Indian Chief of his boyhood, so strangely modified by the Darwinian system of Natural Selection, into a smooth-faced, oily-haired individual clad in paper collar, Eureka shirt, and extensive wide-awake.

The pages of this our second edition, will doubtless, like our first, contain many faults,—and alterations in the times of starting and arrival of trains and boats, will naturally continue to be made, irrespective of us,—without therefore holding ourselves responsible for any such errors, we will promise to endeavor, in future editions, (if the work continues to be as successful as during the first year of its existence,) to make such alterations and corrections as are found necessary from time to time. Any information granted by those best able to afford it—the public—on the *experto crede* principle, will be most readily made use of and acknowledged ; and now once more let us greet all our friends with a hearty

FAREWELL

before terminating our little work with the two words—

THE END.

APPENDIX.

In our first edition, we confined ourselves to the principal places along the "All-Round Route," without diverging either one way or the other,—as, however, in all likelihood, many of our tourists who have never visited the large Western cities, may desire, whilst at Niagara, to take a run even if only for a brief period, to the principal business localities in the Western States; we have thought it desirable, and as a matter of convenience to the travelling public, to refer in a very few words to one or two places in the Western States of America, which are not only worthy, and will amply compensate for any time spent in visiting them, but which really ought to be seen, and well seen, by all those who consider themselves anything of travellers. It is needless to say that we refer to the fine cities of Detroit, in the State of Michigan, and Chicago, in the State of Illinois. A few hours' ride from Suspension Bridge through a pleasant country, over the Great Western Railway, will bring the tourist to the town of Windsor, in Canada, and a few minutes more occupied in crossing the River by the Steam Ferry, will land him in the fine city of Detroit. This city, like most of those in the West, has its principal streets running at right angles, and strangers are at no loss to find their way about. It contains some exceedingly fine buildings, parks and streets. As regards Hotel accommodation, we can confidently recommend the Biddle House, on Jefferson Avenue, as one of the first Hotels in the country, containing all the modern improvements, with every comfort required by the most fastidious. We would advise a visit to the pretty cemetery, and the outskirts of the city, which in all directions are very fine, and will well repay a drive, or a long "constitutional."

As will be anticipated by the tourist, the next and other place which we wish him to visit, is the "New York" of the West, Chicago. Probably most of our pleasure seekers may have already visited the lion city of the West; but to those who have not made the journey within the last few years, we would say, by all means extend your absence from home, and postpone your journey eastward, for at least a few days, and go and see the march of progress being made by our Western friends. Take the Michigan Southern or the Michigan Central Railway at Detroit, and after ten hours of as comfortable travelling as can be obtained on the Continent, you will find yourself in Chicago. Either of the routes named out of Detroit may be selected by the tourist with every confidence, as the time occupied on the journey is about equal, and the scenery along the routes very pleasing.

The Michigan Southern and Northern Indiana Railroad runs from Chicago to Toledo and Detroit,—was completed from Monroe to Hillsdale, 106 miles, in December, 1846, and cars ran through to Chicago, in May, 1852. The total length of the road, and all its branches, is 535 miles. The Depot in Chicago is corner of Van Buren and Sherman streets.

The Michigan Central Road was opened to Kalamazoo, 143 miles from Detroit, February 1st, 1846. The Road was open to Michigan City, October 30, 1850, and to Chicago, May 21, 1852. The total length of the Road is 284 miles. The depot in Chicago is foot of Lake street.

It is truly wonderful, the strides that have been made in Chicago of late years. It is not necessary to recount the particulars of how Chicago has grown in numbers and wealth, within a very limited period; all who have even heard of the place at all, are also acquainted in a greater or lesser degree with the marvellous manner in which the city has risen to its present status, as the Commercial emporium of the West. Chicago, however, must be seen, to be appreciated properly, and one cannot visit the City without feeling that a current of vitality courses through the veins of all its people. As regards Hotels, both the "Tremont" and "Sherman" are fine houses, and our tourist will find every accommodation and comfort at either. There are a number of very fine buildings in the city, and many pleasant drives, but as these are fully enumerated and described in the Guides to the City, published in Chicago, we shall not particularise them.

In returning to the East, if our tourist will spare the time, a most enjoyable and healthful trip may be made by taking the Rail to Milwaukee, and there crossing Lake Michigan by one of the Detroit and Milwaukee Company's very fine steamers to Grand Haven, where they connect with the Railway owned by that Company, running to Detroit. From our own experience we can truly say, that in fine weather this is a most lovely journey, besides varying the route. This will bring our tourist back to Detroit, from whence he will continue his journey on to Niagara (from which point we diverged,) and again join those whom we are escorting on the "All-Round Route Excursion."

RATES OF FARE FROM NIAGARA FALLS—Continued.

DESTINATION.	ROUTE.	Thr'ugh Fare from Niagara Falls.
CRAWFORD HOUSE........	Via Montreal, St. Johns, White River Junction, Wells River and Littleton.......	29.00
Do.	" Ogdensburg, St. Albans, White River Junction, Wells River and Littleton.	23.50
KINGSTON	" Rail or Steamer............	8.50
MONTREAL.................	" Rail or Steamer...........	14.00
NEW YORK.................	" Montreal, Plattsburg, Lake Champlain, Lake George, Saratoga & Hudson River R.R.................	29.50
Do.	" Montreal, Plattsburg, Lake Champlain, Lake George, Saratoga & People's Line of Steamers.............	28.40
Do.	" Montreal, Plattsburg, Lake Champlain, Whitehall, Saratoga and Hudson River R.R.................	26.60
Do.	" Montreal, Plattsburg, Lake Champlain, Whitehall, Saratoga and People's Line of Steamers.............	25.50
Do.	" Montreal, Gorham, Portland, and Boston.............	28.00
Do.	" Montreal, Quebec, Gorham, Portland and Boston......	31.00
Do.	" Montreal, Plattsburg, Lake Champlain, Lake George, Saratoga and Day Line Steamers.................	28.40
Do.	" Montreal, Plattsburg, Lake Champlain, Whitehall, Saratoga and Day Line of Steamers.................	25.50
Do.	" Montreal, Quebec, Gorham, over the White Mountains to Littleton, then via Concord, Nashua and Boston,.	49.00
Do.	" Montreal, Quebec, Sherbrooke, Lake Magog to Newport, Littleton, Stages to and from Profile House and Crawford House, then via Concord, Nashua and Boston.............	49.00
Do.	" Montreal, St. Johns, Burlington, Lake Champlain, Whitehall, Saratoga and Day Line Steamers........	25.50

RATES OF FARE FROM NIAGARA FALLS—*Continued.*

DESTINATION.	ROUTE.	Thr'ugh Fare from Niagara Falls.
NEW YORK	Via Montreal, St. Johns, Burlington, Lake Champlain, Lake George, Saratoga and Day Line Steamers	28.40
Do.	" Ogdensburg, St. Albans, Burlington, Lake Champlain, Whitehall, Saratoga and Day Line Steamers	21.50
Do.	" Ogdensburg, St. Albans, Burlington, Lake Champlain, Lake George, Saratoga and Day Line Steamers	24.40
Do.	" Montreal, St. Johns, White River Junction and Springfield	24.00
Do.	" Ogdensburg, St. Albans, White River Junction and Springfield	20.00
OGDENSBURG	" Rail or Steamer	10.50
PRESCOTT	" Rail or Steamer,	10.50
PORTLAND	" Montreal, Quebec & Gorham.	24.00
Do.	" Montreal and Gorham direct.	21.00
Do. & back to N. FALLS	" Montreal and Gorham, and return by G. T. R.	30.00
PROFILE HOUSE	" Montreal, St. Johns, White River Junction, Wells River, and Stage from Littleton	24.00
Do.	" Ogdensburg, St. Albans, White River Junction, Wells Riv., and Stage from Littleton	20.00
QUEBEC	" Rail or Steamer,	16.50
Do. and back to MONTREAL.	" Rail or Steamer	19.00
SARATOGA	" Montreal, Plattsburg, Lake Champlain & Lake George	24.50
Do.	" Montreal, Plattsburg, Lake Champlain and Whitehall.	21.65
Do.	" Montreal, Gorham, Stages from Alpine House to Glen House, Crawford House, Profile House and Littleton, then Rail to White River Junction and Burlington, and via Lake Champlain & Lake George and Moreau Station to Saratoga	47.75
Do.	" Montreal, St. Johns, Burlington, Lake Champlain and Whitehall	21.65

RATES OF FARE FROM NIAGARA FALLS—*Continued.*

DESTINATION.	ROUTE.	Thr'ugh Fare from Niagara Falls.
SARATOGA	Via Montreal, St. Johns, Burlington, Lake Champlain and Lake George	24.50
Do.	" Ogdensburg, St. Albans, Burlington, Lake Champlain and Whitehall	17.65
Do.	" Ogdensburg, St. Albans, Burlington, Lake Champlain and Lake George	20.50
MONTREAL to QUEBEC and back	" Rail or Steamer	5.00
RICHMOND to QUEBEC and back	" G. T. R.	3.00

The Coupons between Niagara Falls and Toronto, Toronto and Kingston, **Kingston and Prescott, Prescott and** Montreal, **and** Montreal and Quebec, **are valid either** by Boat **or Rail,** and they are **likewise** good by either the **South** Shore Express Line **of** Steamers or by the Royal Mail Line, which **continues** to run **from** Toronto **as** heretofore.

The Tickets include Meals **and** State-rooms on Lake Ontario and the River St. Lawrence, as far as Montreal, but between Montreal and Quebec **they** are for Passage only.

No deviation from the above Rates will be allowed without special authority.

HENRY SHACKELL,
General Passenger Agent G. T. R.

MONTREAL, May 10th, 1869.

www.ingramcontent.com/pod-product-compliance
Lightning Source LLC
Chambersburg PA
CBHW030410170426
43202CB00010B/1551